The States Through Irish Eyes

TWO SORROWING SMALL WHITE LADIES (*page* 156)

THE STATES
THROUGH IRISH EYES

BY

E. Œ. SOMERVILLE

Joint-Author, with Martin Ross
*Of 'Some Experiences of an Irish R. M.,' 'Irish Memories,'
'The Real Charlotte,' etc., etc.*

ILLUSTRATED BY THE AUTHOR

BOSTON AND NEW YORK
HOUGHTON MIFFLIN COMPANY
The Riverside Press Cambridge
1930

The Riverside Press
CAMBRIDGE · MASSACHUSETTS
PRINTED IN THE U.S.A.

ILLUSTRATIONS

THE STATES THROUGH IRISH EYES

. .

CHAPTER I

IT IS reported of John Gilpin, in the matter of that somewhat blighted expedition from London Town to the Bell at Edmonton, that

'He little dreamt when he set out
Of running such a rig.'

Thus it was with me, in, at all events, the preliminary details, when the interesting project of visiting the United States first entered for me the sphere of practical politics. I cannot claim, like John Gilpin, to be 'a citizen of credit and renown,' yet I expected that to take a road so well trodden as that from Ireland to

America, would be a simple matter for an Irish-woman who believed herself to be known not unfavourably to the Police. (Had not, one fine summer's day, a courteous Civic Guard asked permission to regard my sketch, and then, saluting, retired, murmuring ''Tis reality indeed!')

None the less, the first necessity was a visa for the U.S.A., an affair that demanded a journey of some seventy miles, and the presentation in person to the representative of the United States of a well and truly made passport. This last I already possessed, and it had proved its fighting value in many an European contest; but faultless though it admittedly was, it was powerless to allay official suspicion. The door to the Promised Land could not yet be opened to me or to my sister, who had consented to make with me a plunge into the New World.

She, a person blameless as I, if not even more so, had with me to acknowledge that though Aliens (and there is something dark and undesirable in such a definition) we were neither Polygamists nor Anarchists. We had to give an assurance that we had no intention

2

of assassinating any Public Official — not even the Head of the Customs. And enquiries, suggesting a sinister and acrobatic activity, as to 'stock from which Aliens sprang,' and demands as to whether our earlier years had been spent in prisons or lunatic asylums, had all to be carefully responded to.

Then when the United States Government officials had finished with us, the steamer authorities began to occupy themselves with our baggage. How many articles did we possess? What was their individual weight? What their contents? Gasoline? Fireworks? Gunpowder? Movie-films? We stated that we proposed (reluctantly) to leave these at home. The examination moved on to put insoluble problems in connection with our personal or cabin baggages — such as in Virginia I gratefully learnt to call 'go-pokes' (go, to travel; poke, a bag). Had we, or had we not, more than twenty cubic feet of them?...

I thought, with envy, of a tale that had been told to me of a young emigrant to the States from my County of Cork, such an one as I have heard described as a Big Fat Strong Lump of a Counthry-gerr'l. My informant was standing

3

near, and the young emigrant was leaning over
the vessel's side, awaiting the moment of
starting. A boat, piled with a variety of such
things as might appeal to emigrants, came
alongside the big steamer. The boatman
looked up and saw the girl and shouted to her:

'Hi! Miss! D'ye want a thrunk?'

Miss shouted back

'What'd I want a thrunk for?'

'To put your clothes in, sure!'

'And ye'd have me go naked?' says Miss,
unanswerably.

How enviable was her state! A few trifles
enclosed in brown paper, and Peace by sea and
land. A Peace that for such as us passes under-
standing and is certainly not of this world.

.   .   .   .

Cork Harbour was far behind. We had
passed the Old Head of Kinsale, and the Gally
Head. Then came Castlehaven Harbour, and
a tall pillar of brown smoke, bending away to
the eastward before the strong west wind.
That meant Home, and told that there were
those who had forsaken church this bleak
Sunday morning to send us a last greeting
across the grey sea. We borrowed field-glasses

4

and strained our eyes in vain effort to see the fire-makers round the old cairn of stones on which we were sure the farewell pyre was flaming. Nothing was visible. But once two tiny grains of rice seemed to flit across the field of vision. Were they the two little sad dogs, Taspy and Prinkie, whom we had left, standing in profoundest gloom, on the hall-door steps? We trusted so, and that a cliff-rabbit might, in some faint degree, be proving a consolatory substitute for us.

Soon the friendly bonfires died in distance, and then came Cape Clear and the Fastnet Lighthouse and, after they were left behind, nothing but dark grey hills and valleys of water. We said to each other that if we had been Christopher Columbus, we would, at about this point, have put down the helm and run back with a fair wind to Spain. Unfortunately for me, my hat also held this opinion, and, biding its time, it dragged its moorings and hurried back to Ireland, sped by the favouring blast, riding the waves like a thing of life, enviably undistressed by their agitations.

.   .   .   .

I have made but two voyages in those great

5

ships that, like Oscar Wilde, think little of the Atlantic, yet even this limited experience encourages me in the conjecture that those who are officially entitled First Class Passengers have something of the eternal quality of a running brook, for ever moving on, for ever changing, for ever the same. I believe that the Pursers, those experts in diplomacy, who glide like psychological sheepdogs through the social life of Liners, compelling their submissive flock one night to dance, another to make music, another to gamble on the dice-inspired capers of wooden horses, would agree that, taking one trip with another, *plus ça change, plus c'est la même chose.*

One may be reasonably certain that, at this moment, on the promenade decks of any of the big Liners there may be seen identical couples of swift determined women fulfilling their self-appointed task of exercise, striding the length of the long ship, their lips moving as they count their steps, adhering implacably to a cast-iron resolve to walk a prescribed distance daily. Thus also (I am sure) would be found duplicates of the stout pink youth, embodiment of British heartiness and cold salt-

6

water baths, who made the passage with us. He was astir early and sang as he tramped the deck on to which our cabin windows gave. 'Killarney' was the song he most favoured, undaunted by the fact that the high note was never quite within his reach.

Aboard our ship, also, I recall, and with much pleasure, three tall Irish priests, off on a holiday trip to the States, beaming with enjoyment, full of secret jests together, and given to convulsive bursts of tenor laughter, which they suppressed with difficulty, when the two spectacled and coiffed Sisters of Mercy came forth to take the air, bringing with them, as they paced softly to and fro, the restrained atmosphere of the convent garden; while motionless behind the deck-walkers, is ever a long silent row of mummies, laid out in *chaises-longues* and wrapped in rugs, each aloof from the world as was Simeon Stylites on his pillar, but (remembering the rugs and the *chaises-longues*) in no other way resembling him.

There came an evening, the last, I think, that we were to spend in the ship, when it was officially decreed that we were to lift up our hearts and feature gaiety. To facilitate this

7

effort, all were provided with tissue-paper head-gear in a vast variety of form and colour. On the small table allotted to my sister and me were two folded layers of paper, emerald green and pink respectively. One developed into a biretta with a long jewelled plume, the other became a sunbonnet. We assumed them with a profound reluctance, and began gloomily upon the soup, with downcast eyes, fearing to look upon each other.

'"Let us be merry," said Mr. Pecksniff. Here he took a captain biscuit.'

CHAPTER II

IT IS, I know, incumbent on all visitors to the
United States to experience, on their first sight
of New York's silhouette, very definite reactions, and subsequently to dilate upon them.
The Statue of Liberty, also, seems to be regarded as a sort of test of artistic sensibility.
I was told of a Frenchman who, on being asked
what he thought of the lady, replied (with,
possibly, a passing thought of Prohibition)
that he was interested to find that in America
as in Europe, monuments were raised to the
illustrious dead. But we were spared the re-
sponsibilities of either reactions or epigrams, as
a dense fog smothered the famous skyline, and
Liberty was not only dead but buried in its wet
folds.

I had asked a travelled friend to sketch

lightly for me the conditions that govern arrival at the docks in New York. She replied concisely

'Hell and Bedlam.'

Intimidated by this, we lingered in the good ship 'Cedric,' that had now become a home, and when, almost the last of the voyagers, we took the hooded way to the New World, we were received not only by a faithful gathering of friends, but with what is called, with Old World elegance, 'The Courtesy of the Port.' Neither Hell nor Bedlam was suggested by this vast, dim place, almost desolately empty — we had indeed been the last to leave the ship — where the courtesy of the Port was matched by the courtesy of the porters.

Not thus do my fellow countrymen at the portals of Erin receive a stranger! There, I regret to admit, Customs have mastered manners. I have heard of a blameless traveller, innocent of tobacco, spirits, or even American clocks (all in a common and obscure condemnation) who had to pay duty on the possession of six shirts.

'What'd anny man want with more than two?' was the official opinion.

10

A lady of my acquaintance, maddened by the sight of her carefully packed garments being churned by the rude and unclean hands of an underling, demanded of him information as to what he was looking for.

Continuing to churn, he replied, smilingly, 'Begorra, I don't know!'

.   .   .   .

Our arrangements had decreed that our first visit to New York should be a very brief one, and it passed like a flash, a luxurious, almost, I might say, a padded flash. Save to cross a sidewalk, foot of ours was never set to ground. Seated serenely in our hostess's car, we learnt what it was to race the red light from block to block, staring at the streets whose names were so familiar, finding it hard to believe that we had actually seen Broadway, and Wall Street, and that this was Fifth Avenue.

Outstanding is the memory of a visit to the magnificent Morgan Library, made under the sheltering wing of a lady very specially qualified to expound its treasures to the ignorant and unlearned. Outstanding also is a Philharmonic Concert, and Signor Toscanini's grey curls shaking in the wind of his wrath, as,

11

bâton in hand, he denounced the stricken party of late-comers — (not us, safely planted in a box) — crawling up the central aisle with the eyes of the house upon them.

I ask myself what else did we do in New York? And the answer is — what did we not do! Memory responds with a blurred dazzle of dinners, and lunches, and introductions to charming people, introductions made, usually, in a storm of conversation, and that, as is also usual, introduced me to one name only, my own. And with all these, studios, and picture-galleries, and theatre-parties, and, very nearly, a visit to the Nethermost Pit, by way of a chasm that had opened in the road near one theatre, and challenged comparison with the worst type of County Cork bog-hole.

Some one has said that New York is like a woman wearing a tiara of diamonds, and with her bare feet showing through the holes in her boots. We had certainly seen one of the holes, but I make haste to say that the trope as to the tiara was, later on, equally justified and ex-emplified in (beyond, I think, all other won-ders) the glories of the Railway Stations.

These had, however, yet to be revealed to

us as our visit to Long Island was smoothly achieved by road. I suppose the selvage or raw edge of any great city is not meant to be seen, but it is not fortunate that in order to accomplish a visit to the beauties and super-civilisation of Long Island, it is necessary on leaving New York to drive through the heart of what looks like a gigantic ashpit.

'Don't look at anything!' said our hostess-chauffeur, with a firm foot on the accelerator.

We obeyed. As a matter of fact, at X, (an unknown quantity) m.p.h., one can only close the eyes and pray.

.   .   .   .

It is my intention, perhaps I should say my ambition, to keep these casual impressions impersonal, having realised (thanks to certain examples) that between persons and personalities there is but 'the little more, and how much it is!' I will therefore only say of our stay in Long Island and our experiences there, that the reactions inspired were entirely enjoyable and of the sort that endure. But I may tell of a visit to a great stable of hunters, among whom was one that I had never thought to see again — Brian, the last colt that Kitty, my last and almost best loved hunter-mare, had left to me.

In allotting to Kitty this responsible position memory recalls, not without some slight reproach, other high lights of my stables, some of whom I have already commemorated elsewhere, but I may be forgiven for once more mentioning Bridget, who, if she viewed the fox before I did, would fling back her 'wise little, grey little head,' and administer to my leg a warning thump. Or Lady Meath, with the manners of a high-born Abbess, and a mouth so light that one could ride her 'with a sop o' hay for a bit'; of whom, with a spiteful eye on her fired fore-legs, a jealous cynic said 'Without them she'd not be in Carbery!' But Kitty, with her petulant fine-lady airs, and her capricious indecisions as to whether this were or were not one of her days to be afraid of jumping stones (so that it was well said of her that the way it was when you'd be riding that mare, it was better for you to have no patience, for if you had you'd lose it) and yet, when she chose, so adorable, so stylish, so perfect an artist over any country, that a member of my Hunt told me I must never fail to wear a top-hat when

14

I rode her — Kitty is in a class by herself.

The remembrance of her charms has beguiled me, and I have wandered away from her tall brown son, and from that visit to him that came so near to being left unpaid. We had timed it badly, and arriving, as it befell, at the stablemen's dinner hour, there was no one to receive us but the resident dog, an animal bristling with hostility, that I was told was a Schnauzer. I have since learned that Schnauzers are a definite breed that is rapidly becoming fashionable. At the moment, however, I had never heard of such. It seemed to me that the guardian of the stables was the result of a mesalliance between a brindled bulldog and a Kerry Blue terrier, and remembering that I had been told in Kerry that a Kerry Blue was not bred from unless he had either killed his enemy in battle, or been killed himself, I did not leave the car. Happily, the thought of the men's dinner hour just then occurred to the Schnauzer, and, still growling, he retired.

It was disappointing that the colt had forgotten me. When, a little later, he was paraded

15

for my inspection, he was as distant and self-engrossed as horses are wont to be when their visitors are able to produce nothing that is edible.

CHAPTER III

OUR time in Long Island was unavoidably short, and we had to forego the pleasure of a visit to the Meadowbrook Kennels. But we saw something of the country the hounds hunt over, and what we beheld filled us with respect, even with awe. They hunt wild foxes, and the coverts are set among great grass fields that are divided by 'obstackles' of a size and ferocity that are, one would say, rarely equalled. Barricades of heavy timber of from four to five feet high, that pose as the humble and comparatively fragile post and rail, calculated to turn over any horse that 'leaves an iron' on them, and to turn also any save the stoutest heart to water. It is a common weakness that strange countries, with few exceptions, look

17

to the anxious visitor, unrideable, but it seems to me that the biggest 'double' in Meath, or the tallest wall in Galway would be less alarming to most Irish riders than the average Long Island 'timber'; and when one reflects that there is nothing to check hounds, who can slide between or under the great bars without, hardly, breaking their stride, one feels that an active kangaroo would be the only mount capable of inspiring confidence.

. . . .

American country-houses have — as far as my fairly extended experience goes — a very distinct *cachet* of their own. There is, to begin with, the attractive quality of unexpectedness. They observe no conventions. Each house is a law to itself. In one of them, perhaps, you find the living-place is a great, irregular-shaped hall, with a vast mediæval fireplace, and with special facilities for what may be called limited-group — (which includes tête-à-tête) — sociabilities; and there may be a wide staircase that flings out branches of lesser flights of steps, stimulating the imagination with their suggestions of regions yet to be explored.

You tell yourself that you have found your

18

ideal, yet at the next home to which you are introduced, you may be led along a broad corridor, to discover your hostess in a delightful hybrid between a drawing-room and a conservatory, while the other living-rooms lead from it in level and stately procession, and you find yourself developing a fresh ideal. Moreover, it was borne in upon us, deflated Queens of Sheba, with the spirit quite crushed out of us by the sight of these marvellous houses, so attractive and so expensive, that more than money went to their making, and that American architects and home-makers were depressingly endowed with talent and good taste. Depressing from our point of view, because in Ireland we have no architecture. Some few respectable and comfortable old Georgian mansions there may be, still unburnt, and there are Norman castles that will gratify the tourist by frowning as Norman Castles should; but we have but little to boast of in the matter of cathedrals and churches, and the best that can be said for our buildings is that they are typically Irish in their disdain for externals, — ('I'm too grand to be grand!' said an old Galway lady of exalted lineage and extreme per-

19

sonal untidiness) — and they show a common respect for that great economic maxim, 'If it'll do, it'll do!'

. . . .

So it was that two humble Irish explorers stood amazed at the variety of type and ingenuity of design of the myriad buildings, whether tiny bungalow or gorgeous Country Club, that they beheld, as they pursued their instructive course from State to State. We regarded wistfully their attractive proportions, their pillared verandahs, and knew, with a yearning jealousy, that even as day follows night, so had each bedroom its satellite bathroom, with its shining tiles of virgin white, and its twin Niagaras, tamed to every day's most common need, H. and C. combining simultaneously and miraculously to deliver the perfect bath, and we sighed, and thought of the community-bathroom of many a British home, and said that great as is the American architect, the Crown of America is the Plumber.

. . . .

It occurs to me that now, while I am meditating upon American architecture, is the moment to make a protest that the subject suggests. I have heard that in China if a well-bred person wishes to enquire of another the extent of his family, the enquiry should be posed something in this wise:

'How many honourable princes has the nobleman to whom I address myself?'

And the nobleman will respond

'This degraded person has five little dogs!'

Similarly in America, when a fine and venerable mansion, standing amid ancient trees, moved us to the admiring respect due to dignified old age, we were immediately assured that to us it must have the air of a mushroom — if not a toad-stool. While to us, on the other hand, remembering Charleston with its beautiful old buildings, and its stormy history of three hundred years, or Boston, with the serious elderly magnificence of Beacon Street, or Providence, with its old colonial mansions, and streets whose names bring delightfully to mind the Pilgrim's Progress and the City of Mansoul, the title of 'The New World' seemed an affectation, an elegant gesture of humility that was quite out of place.

. . . .

It was somewhat restoring to our Old World

self-esteem to find that the American genius for architecture did not seem to take much account of churches. In such country villages as we visited, or were whirled through, in the course of our wanderings, the design of the churches was apparently inspired by that of the primitive toy-shop Noah's Ark; in the towns it is the sky-scrapers that point the way to heaven — (in fact go a long way toward getting there) — dwarfing the spires and towers whose mission they have usurped.

That there are some ancient places of worship may be deduced from a tale that was bestowed on me by a friend in Boston. A carpenter was mending the floor of one of the high-sided square pews in a New England church of the time of Queen Anne. There entered two tourist ladies of the sight-seeing type, whose peculiarities of behaviour (notably in foreign churches) Miss Ruth Draper has collected and impaled on a very sharp pin for our instruction and entertainment. These, having explored the building to their satisfaction, consulted together as to the indispensable 'souvenir.' Their eagle glances swept the empty church and alighted upon a fine and very old

Bible that was on the reading-desk. They told each other, happily, that a leaf from this historic relic would be just right, and they were advancing upon the Bible, when the carpenter, concealed under the seat of the pew, shouted in a terrible voice 'What the hell are you doin' there?'

The alarmed ladies, abandoning the proposed souvenir, rushed from the church.

'I guess,' said the carpenter reflectively, in subsequent narration, 'I guess they thought it was the Voice of Gawd!'

CHAPTER IV[1]

I_T_ is time that our gratitude and admiration for the amenities of American travel should be given suitable expression. We were bound for South Carolina, a long night journey into the unknown, but we faced it with the composure bestowed by the possession of 'Reservations,' and of two guardian and highly competent angels, who had undertaken to see us safe out of New York.

Arrived at the Pennsylvania Railway Station, we stood, amazed, on the floor of a building so vast and splendid that it might justifiably resent the comparison with St. Paul's Cathedral that rose to our lips. A flock of red-

[1] By the courtesy of the Editor of 'Vogue,' this, and the following chapter, are, with some alterations, omissions, and additions, reprinted from that paper.

capped, black-faced porters swooped down on us and our monstrous regiment of trunks and go-pokes. They looked to us like exotic birds. It seemed impossible that they could understand our language or follow our instructions. Nor did they. We had to follow theirs. We did so abjectly, faintly trusting the larger hope that we should again, in this world, meet the things with which the Red-caps had flown away. The Guardian Angels, smiling at our anxieties, led us to the Restaurant, promising that all would be well.

And so, presently, we found ourselves, and a generous selection of go-pokes, safely established in a 'drawing-room' compartment of a long train for the South. No *wagon-lit* accommodation in European trains could compare with the comfort of the 'drawing-room' apportioned to us. Large, airy, with immense windows, and generously endowed with gadgets, electric and otherwise, to meet every conceivable need of light or heat. Even had the berths been less comfortable than they were, there would have been compensation in the sight of the species of earthquake from whose throes they arose, and having expired as arm-

25

chairs, were reincarnated as beds. Even more interesting and exciting was the method of the coloured attendant in making up the bed of the upper *étage*, which he achieved by flinging at it from below, pillows, sheets, and blankets, with the skill of a Roman retiarius in netting his foe.

In the Restaurant Car, elbow-room such as our British railways deny us, was bestowed for the leisurely consumption of a generous meal. And let me not forget to recall the almost paternal kindness of the youthful white authority among the black minions of the car, who, casting an eye over the repast of two venerable female travellers, inquired, solicitously,

'You gurls fixed all right?'

We began to understand the undismayed calm with which Americans set forth upon journeys by train that may last for three days or more. But — and this is the sole reproach that occurs to me to make — how do their nerves endure the shocks involved by the usually imperceptible operations of stopping or starting the train? When we first heard the grinding roar, and felt the shattering jolt that are involved by arrival at a station, we sprang to our feet and prepared for the worst.

CHAPTER V

EVERYONE knows that it is 'a long, long way to Tipperary,' and the converse holds good, since it is undoubtedly a long way from Tipperary — or even the County of Cork, which is, after all, the jumping-off place — to South Carolina, and it was from South Carolina that had come the invitation that had brought us across the ocean.

But at last, on a rainy morning, two hours late, thanks to a prolonged pause during the night in a pitch-dark siding at Washington, (a by-product, we understood, of President Hoover's Inauguration which had occurred that day,) at long last, after strenuous journeyings by sea and land, we reached our goal, Aiken.

And in spite of the rain and the delayed arrival, there were friends and flowers waiting to greet us! How wonderful to find a dream come true, and the reality more wonderful than the dream! And this was what happened to me and my sister.

. . . .

Aiken, S.C., is a place that may have its parallel in America, but is certainly unique in my experience. With its perfect winter and spring climate, its gardens and woods, it is an ideal Pleasure-place, but preëminently it is a place devoted to the worship of the Horse, in all his moods and tenses. Hunting, Racing, Polo, Coaching, the cults are many, but all do homage at the same shrine. Around the select and original circle of worshippers, others less concentrated, more prone to go astray after false gods, (such as Golf, Lawn Tennis, Clay-pigeon-shooting, or even Bridge) have gathered, but these frivolities, even though tolerated, possibly even partaken in by the elect, are of quite secondary importance. 'They,' as Lord Bacon said of garden devices of which he disapproved, 'They be but toys,' the Horse is (and very properly) the tutelary deity of Aiken.

Amongst the differing cults I see I have

omitted to mention Buggy-driving, and the omission must be repaired, as I consider that to drive, or even to retain one's seat, in an Aiken buggy, in Aiken Woods, is an infinitely more searching test of both skill and nerve than is afforded by any other method of getting over the ground on wheels. That, at least, (as I shall presently endeavour to expound) became my opinion after my first experience of following the Aiken Draghounds, in an Aiken buggy, through Aiken Woods, and I have seen no reason to change it.

.   .   .   .

It was my sister's and my great good fortune to be the guests of the house that is the centre and mainspring of all that makes Aiken so enchanting a playground. Earlier in these simple annals I have declared, and, as I thought, firmly, that neither persons nor personalities should have place in them; but consistency is a weakness — 'the hobgoblin of small minds' George Meredith says — A Personage is quite another affair, and to speak of Aiken and not to mention Mrs. Thomas Hitchcock, would be like playing 'Hamlet' without the Prince of Denmark.

To begin with, she is the Master of the celebrated Aiken Draghounds (as well as of a sporting little pack of stud-book Beagles) and the Hunt is the outstanding feature in the social life of this crowded colony of sportsmen and sportswomen. But to attempt to tell of all that Mr. and Mrs. Hitchcock have done and do for sport in general, and for the cult of the thoroughbred horse in particular, is a task, grateful though it would be, that is beyond the scope of these random impressions.

More within my power is it to narrate the strictly personal experiences of two neophytes in buggy-driving, who, though fairly competent in the conduct of an Irish jaunting-car, were quite unversed in the manners and customs of buggies.

A perfect specimen of the breed had been generously (I had almost said recklessly) placed at our disposal by our hostess, and on the gay and sunshiny morning that followed our arrival, we rose to find our private and personal buggy awaiting us on the sandy road by the stables. It was our first sight of a buggy, and we surveyed the equipage with excitement not unmixed with apprehension. A long-legged brown horse was in the shafts, a small brown boy stood at — or as near as he could reach to — the horse's head. The buggy looked fragile, not to say spectral — a sort of anatomical study of what had once been a mail-phaëton. Very delicately we climbed in, and felt, when we had fitted ourselves cautiously into the seat, like two large spiders precariously poised in a web that was very far from being up to their weight.

I took the reins in my hand, my sister grasped the side rail in hers; the small brown boy, whose impressive name was found to be Nathaniel, adhered, impossible to say how, to some aftermost and outlying strand of the web behind us, and we were off.

We had been directed as to the road through the woods by which the hounds had preceded us, and, turning aside from the main road, we addressed the brown horse to it. He seemed to be a long way from us, and his connection with the buggy of the most tenuous. He flitted rapidly before us, like a domesticated Daddy Longlegs, and the buggy pursued him ir-relevantly and at varying angles. We should have preferred to go very slowly, but having

31

heard — it was long ago, at the Dublin Horse Show, watching Driving Competitions — that the more an American trotting-horse's mouth is pulled the faster he goes, we thought it best to let him determine the rate of speed.

Our way lay through virgin forest, through which on this fair morning, delicious shafts of sunlight pierced their path. They fell at intervals on the road, and the more we saw (and felt) of its surface, the more uncertainty beset us; it seemed that we must have missed the way, that it was impossible that wheels were expected to traverse this alarming, this almost incredible combination of eminences and ravines. But Daddy Longlegs slopped along at a steady trot, and the buggy hopped after him without protest, and we thought of the Honour of Ireland and sat tight—or as tight as we could.

. At length reassurance that we were on the right road came with the sight of a couple of hounds; they were investigating the undergrowth between the pine trees. Then came the familiar sound of a whip cracking, followed by a 'rate' at the stragglers, and a smart young Whip came galloping towards us and put her charges on with professional severity. At the

32

next turn of the track all was well, the hounds were in sight, eight or ten useful-looking couples jogging along in charge of a remarkably well turned out and beautifully mounted amateur Hunt Staff. Mr. Hitchcock was Acting-Master and Huntsman that day, and a lad and two lasses formed his zealous and competent staff. Not often have I seen girls ride astride with as perfect a command of their horses and as easy and graceful a seat as had these girls, and still more unusual for us was the sight of a Hunt Staff all riding thorough-breds.

I must confess that I find it impossible to see such horses as these without an acute spasm of covetousness, but when, that morning, the first admiring, yearning throb had subsided, I thought of the hills of West Carbery, the rocky staircases, the slatey ledges half hidden in furze, the fences that exact the caution, the deliberation, and the governed activity of a cat, and decided that to each country its own, and enviable as were the Aiken hunt horses, I would not care to follow hounds on them over Lough Ine Hill!

But to follow them through the Aiken Woods

33

was a different matter; the green coats, the white breeches, the velvet caps, and the shining long-tailed blood horses made a lovely and ever-changing picture as they jogged ahead of us, leading the way between the crowding pine trees along the track whose warm red-orange sand supplied just the colour needed to make the picture perfect. The tall pines were all hung with garlands of jasmin, green, then, in the beginning of March. Far south though we were, the time of their yellow blossoms was not yet. A small lake brought light on this sunny morning into the shade of the forest. At intervals, long openings between the trees showed where the different Lines for the different Drags had their courses. Every moment riders and buggies, coming by devious ways through the vast woods, joined the procession. I think it was about half way to the Meet that the privilege became mine of occupying a seat in the Master's buggy, in which she was driving herself, the tyranny of a broken leg having temporarily condemned her to follow her hounds on wheels, instead of, as is her wont, heading the Hunt on horseback. My place in our buggy was given to a young fellow-visitor, and my sister, into whose hands he was entrusted, was instructed to follow implicitly the lead of the Master.

It was a mild and delicious day, and the throng of riders and drivers grew ever more dense. Presently came the dividing of the ways, the separation of the sheep, as represented by the buggies, from the goats, those whose agility would soon be proved by the grim tests offered by the jumps of the Drag Line. But an agility scarcely less high was demanded of the sheep. If the drivers were to see the finish they had no time to lose.

'Oh Life! Oh Time!' says Shelley, classing them as equals. But with the followers of the Aiken Drag, Life, as compared with Time, is a small thing. The buggies, released from the restraint of the hounds' jog, sprang into ferocious activity. Through the boiling yellow flood of the Sand River, heedless of holes, and the unseen traps of submerged branches, we dashed at full speed. The track — I cannot call it a road — offered a variety of perils no less serious, but a given spot had to be reached in a given time, and the Leader of the buggies recked little of perils.

35

One has heard of the Irishman whose trousers were made of holes tied together with bits of string. There are times, after seasons of heavy rain, when the ways through the Aiken Woods appear — to the visitor — to consist of crevasses linked together by ropes of sand. This was such a period. The Master's buggy sped onwards, now leaping the crevasses, now exploring their depths. There were moments when the remembrance of Korah, Dathan, and Abiram, who, we are told, went 'quick into the pit' and reappeared no more, was almost overpowering. But the Honour of Ireland had to be maintained. I clutched the side rail convulsively and said nothing, only casting an occasional eye backwards to see how my sister and her companion, close behind us, were faring. Her jaw was set, her companion's expression was strained, Daddy Longlegs had laid himself out to go, and was obviously pulling hard, but they were following in comparatively good order, and the rest of the buggies pressed hard after them.

Suddenly, and with — it cannot be concealed — immeasurable relief, I saw that our way was blocked by an immense fallen tree.

36

Dense thickets of sapling trees surrounded us, and on one side a steepish slope, thick-set with young trees, ended in a deep and boggy ditch. Here, I thought, this Tam-o'-Shanter effort will cease. How little I then knew the Master of the Aiken Draghounds! Unhesitating, she spun round her buggy on a single wheel, and plunged through the undergrowth down into the boggy ditch. A hand-to-hand encounter between a stout young oak and the axle of the buggy ensued, the remainder of that indomitable vehicle standing on its tail in the ditch, while the mare, high above us on the farther side, being not without experience in such crises, knew her duty and did it.

Sooner than had seemed possible the young oak yielded, and then, trampling down the young trees before it, the Master's buggy sprang forward and the impossible had been achieved.

My sister asserts that Daddy Longlegs proved good, and that she and her young charge followed in our track. As to this I cannot say. 'The pace,' as 'Nimrod' says, 'was too good to enquire.' I know only that the position which had been stormed with such

37

intrepidity was one that gave access to a spot that permitted a perfect view of the tall and stiff brushwood fence that was the finish of to-day's Drag. We had reached it to the very moment. The hounds fleeted by us, conscientiously crying their quest and 'passed in music out of sight.' Then, up the broad grassy track cut through the trees, came the thrilling sound of the drumming of many hoofs, and in another instant the riders were flashing by us, charging the fence at Grand National speed, headed by the green coats of the Hunt.

Drags that are frankly drags, and not perfidious, aniseeded imitations of fox-hunts — (a temptation to which I have known usually upright sportsmen to yield in order to ensure a gallop for an unsuspecting stranger) — these acknowledged drag-hunts have an irresponsible habit of developing into steeplechases. These hard-going, not to say dare-devil, riders of Aiken had galloped, 'Hell-for-leather,' for three miles, and had crossed as many fences to the mile as even West Carbery could offer, and now they were coming at that final and formidable fence uphill. But not a horse checked. Out of his stride each swept over the big jump,

38

and not a rider, down to the youngest lad of them, so much as stirred in his saddle.

When I look back on our visit to Aiken, all is merged in a sunny whirl of hospitalities and excitements. Polo at one of the many polo-grounds, lawn-tennis, field-trials, clay-pigeon-shooting, a drive in a smart four-in-hand, luncheons, teas, and dinners, all as agreeable as they were unceasing! The heads of the two strangers within Aiken's gates were fairly turned by the warmth of the welcome that was given to them.

Impossible to tell of all the 'divarsions,' but the remembrance of one especial dinner-party is ineffaceable. It was a very sporting affair. Our host was an M.F.H., one of the foremost of American sportsmen, and well known in Ireland as well as in his own country, and other Masters of Hounds, present and past, were among the guests. I can see now the long low room, with its many silver tokens of Racing and Horse-Show triumphs, its walls hung with fine old sporting prints. And the picture is before my eyes of the glittering lighted table and the gay and beaming faces round it, and the host in his scarlet evening coat, with his

39

keen huntsman's face, and his silver astrakan head, wielding a carving knife that looked as though it had begun life as a cavalry sabre, operating with it, with amazing dexterity, upon two gigantic turkeys, that must have measured seventeen hands at the withers (or perhaps I should say the wattles) and were, nevertheless, as tender as spring chickens.

And the Talk! No simile that I can think of, no kennel of hounds at feeding time, no Jazz-Band in delirium tremens, ever equalled that supreme and jovial row!

.   .   .   .

One other recollection cannot be left untold — the Hunt Breakfast, and the Barbecue! But such a hunt breakfast! It followed on a drag-run that was of more than usual severity, being the weekly fixture dedicated by the Master to 'l'éducation sportive' of the boys and girls of the two famous Aiken schools, of whom some forty or fifty had come out, all well-mounted, and riding with the demon-jealousy proper to youth. The run over, the rush of the buggies in a single direction, darting like woodcock through the trees instead of dispersing in the usual more leisurely fashion, told of some hap-

40

pening out of the common. And told the truth. In a clearing in the heart of the forest we came upon two long tables, set for near two hundred guests; near them, in charge of dark experts in primitive cookery, the Barbecue!

The hospitality of the Master of the Aiken Hunt is in the great tradition of the South. Two lambs and a young pig, roasting whole, over a single huge wood fire in a sandy trough, were only incidents in that woodland feast. The staff-work that the organisation of such a picnic, on such a scale, must have involved was marvellous in its efficiency. The buggies were moored intricately, among the trees, and we sat down seriously to the lambs and the young pig. After these *pièces de résistance* followed one of the masterpieces of Creole cookery, known, mysteriously, as 'Hopping John'; an admirable confection, something of the nature of a Pilaff, but composed of ingredients that defied identification (which is, in my view, the crowning merit of good cookery), and then the super-civilised finish to this barbaric feast of perfect ices and coffee.

Finally, the Cake-walk! with strident music from a negro band, hidden in a near-by cot-

tage, hitherto silent, now very much the re-
verse, and six little darkies treading their
measure in perfect time round and round the
company seated at the long tables, the swains
no more than three feet high, with boots nearly
as long as themselves, ogling their simpering
partners over first one shoulder and then the
other; while the young ladies, a little larger
than the gentlemen, arrayed like Solomon in
all his glory, evaded their glances with coquet-
tish turnings of their woolly and bedizened
bullet-heads.

CHAPTER VI

'WHEN we were very young' (as Mr. Milne says) it was our practice while our morning toilet was in progress, to sing — or perhaps I should say, yell — what were then known as 'Christy Minstrel' songs, and we were confident that in so doing we were giving tongue to the joys and sorrows of the American Plantation negro. Later experience has shaken this early belief, but none the less there came, at Aiken, a day when once more I arose and dressed myself to the tune of

'I'm off to Charleston early in de mornin'.'

(Possessing me, as tunes will, circulating in my being as though a perpetual gramophone were functioning at the very root of consciousness.)

The persistent tune had this time some justification, for the time had come to bid a very regretful farewell to Aiken, and it was indeed Charleston for which we proposed to start, and at 8.30 A.M., which, though not strictly '*before the break o' day*,' is quite creditably early in the morning — but not too early for us to find a small company of very special friends waiting on the sunny road to rise our hearts and give us a cheerful send-off.

I do not know why my sister and I, two full-sized persons, in fairly full possession of our senses, should have been wrapped — as it were — in cotton-wool, and handed from one careful hostess to another with precautions and injunctions that were quite out of proportion to our value.

('Annything don't throuble thim!' said the Cork railway-waiting-room woman, surveying my two little dogs, seated on my rug, looking serenely at me, while I slaved about baggage and kindred afflictions.)

Thus it was with us. We were handed on, like a Foreign Office Bag, in continuous safe-keeping. Nothing troubled us; and with the assurance that passive obedience was all that was required of us, we were packed into a large and luxurious 'Lincoln,' and sent forth anew on our travels.

.   .   .   .

Our way from Aiken lay across an immense plain, that stretched, featureless, beyond our vision, under the great circle of sky. Cultivation everywhere, not so much as a weed to be seen. How the cultivation had been accomplished was a mystery, if one might judge by the only visible cultivators. At intervals of perhaps a mile, a solitary mule, accompanied by an equally solitary negro, might be discerned, creeping, a speck in the vast landscape, towards the horizon. The task seemed the materialisation of hopelessness. Yet, I repeat, we saw no weeds.

It was a long drive, some hundred and forty miles, from Aiken to where it was appointed we were to be collected by our next caretaker. We were going due south, and we knew it by the steady rise in the temperature as the big car flung the miles behind her. And by the flowers. At Aiken the jasmin and the azaleas and the wistaria had scarcely begun, and not even a dandelion had at first enlivened the bare leagues through which we had whirled. The

45

last miles of the route had been through un-
tamed forest, and the first hint of the amenities
of culture was given by a tree, a forest tree
indeed, but subjugated, overwhelmed, over-
flowed, by a veil of pale wistaria blossoms.
Soon after that came houses, no two alike, save
in their setting of flowering shrubs, azaleas,
rhododendrons, and wistaria wherever it could
find a friend to cling to. The smooth green
lawns on which the houses stood, ran on, in
the neighbourly American way, from one house
to another, with no mark to tell where each
domain began and ended. It implied to us, accustomed to high walls and rigidly maintained
boundaries, a millennial peace and good-fellow-
ship. But what of the dogs? Surely between
the Montagues of 'Wistaria Cottage' and the
Capulets of 'The Azaleas' some frontier de-
fences are required? Yet it would appear that
even the Schnauzers, (that breed ugly and
cross as their name) and 'Police Dogs' (i.e.
Alsatians) must respect each other's privacy
and observe the conditions of the millen-
nium.

Carefully obeying sailing orders, we awaited
collection in the hall of an immense hotel, one

of several in this flowery garden-town, (with a name so familiar to us, even though we might differ over its spelling). It was our first experience of a Southern hotel, and everything spoke of a new and unfamiliar type of civilisation. Black waiters were everywhere. Their shadowy faces had not yet ceased to give us a slight shock of bewilderment, and still appeared to be all exactly alike. At Aiken we had found something very engaging in the gentle coloured voices, and the soft coloured manners, and the care with which a good coloured servant can surround one. Had there been so much as a crumple in a roseleaf, 'Mittie,' to whose care we had been consigned, would have ironed it smooth with the same assiduity that she brought to bear on our evening dresses. But at Summerville we found a different atmosphere. The dark potentate, of whom we enquired as to the possibility of obtaining a cup of coffee, referred us, with chill hauteur, to the 'Desk.' 'The Desk,' with even greater hauteur, gave us to understand that the request was ill-timed. It was unmoved by the intelligence that we had breakfasted at 8.30. According to the Desk, coffee, unattended by

47

lunch, was never required by the Best People. We retired, shamed, to unobtrusive seats behind a long row of large rocking-chairs, in each of which an elderly gentleman was rocking himself, softly and carefully, as though he were a teething baby. Splendid ladies swung to and fro past us, conversing loudly. I would fain have said swept, (a word, in this connection, invariably dedicated to the movement of splendid ladies) but though mere legs cannot be said to sweep, their swinging silken stride was almost equally impressive. They glanced at us, occasionally, as they passed, in a way that made us know that our hats were very wrong and un-American. It was terrible to find how un-American we were. People at Aiken, we realised then, had been too kind to tell us. We promised each other that we would buy thoroughly American hats at the earliest opportunity. Meantime we could only sit there in the background and feel despised.

.   .   .   .

Suddenly our hats were forgotten, and we were plucked from obscurity into sunshine by a Rescuer, who came swiftly and unhesitatingly across the crowded hall to us. (So unhesitatingly as, on reflection, to intensify our distrust of our hats.) She brought with her a new and delightful atmosphere of charm and friendliness. Our self-confidence began to hold up its head. The coloured potentate's hauteur fell from him (almost, one would say, with a crash). He occupied himself zealously with our luggage. (Did I say that we had thirteen pieces, including go-pokes?) The shadowy waiters carried all to the waiting motor, like assiduous crows bearing sticks to their nests. We revived in this new air, so gay, so exhilarating, and a luncheon-basket that 'breathed of the sweet South' in all its delicious details, made us forget the denials of the Desk.

·   ·   ·   ·   ·   ·   ·   ·   ·

One of the first duties of the conscientious visitor to the States is to visit the Charleston Gardens. Of this we were steadily assured by all those who had our instruction and improvement seriously at heart. Such a visit, we gathered, was more than a pleasure; it amounted to being a duty owed to American civilisation; these two achievements, the Middleton Place Gardens and the Magnolia Gardens, being testimonies to a cultivation that is

49

intellectual as well as horticultural, and that has a past of a couple of hundred years and more.

We accepted the obligation with alacrity. We had long since been disabused of the prevalent British conception of America as a country young and crude, with, it is conceded, something to boast of in the Present, and possibly more to look forward to in the Future, but with no Past worthy of the name. I think it must be owing to some obscure 'Humility Complex' that any visible proofs of a respectable antiquity are emphasised, even though in the same breath their importance may be disparaged. And it is possibly for a like reason that conversation between a recently introduced visitor from the Old Country and a citizen of the States, tends to veer towards pedigree, and the forbears of the family whose acquaintance the visitor is making. Yet, after all, in a land that has been overrun with Aliens (such as those anticipated Anarchists and Polygamists from whom we tried to dissociate ourselves), it is reasonable enough to prefer to remember that one's ancestors made the crossing with Sir Walter Raleigh, or in the 'Mayflower,' instead of in the steerage of an emigrant ship!

. . . .

It need scarcely be said that neither of the celebrated gardens was allowed to be 'quite looking its best.' To no garden, as to no child, has this culminating moment ever been known to arrive. None the less, we had not been told too much of the beauty that we were to find, and we found it hard to believe that on this mild and sunny southern day the moment had not actually culminated.

I have heard of a venerable lady who, discussing the appearance of a friend whom she had not met since their schooldays, remarked,

'Well, forty years do make a difference in a girl, don't they?'

It is indisputable; so also is the fact that two hundred years of cultivation do a great deal towards obliterating the primeval jungle. The Middleton Place Gardens have Tradition at their back, and History too, and they live up to their past. The entrance is in the grand style. A broad avenue, with a very wide space of level grass on either hand, bordered by tall trees, goes straight from the gates to the house. Given sufficient greatness in width and length, and given, also, the dignity of tall attendant trees, there is something impressive in a direct approach, that disdains to turn aside, and seeing its objective goes straight for it.

Of the great house that gave the avenue its reason for existence very little remains. It lived through the Revolution. Its owner, Arthur Middleton, was one of the signers of the Declaration of Independence. British troops held it for a time, and treated the beautiful pictures and furniture with the monkey-destructiveness proper to warriors on the warpath. But they, at least, did not burn the house (an oversight that they may have regretted, since, after their defeat, it was in it that the terms were arranged for their departure from Carolina).

Less than a century later, Sherman came

> — '*Buzzin' along to de sea,*
> *Like Moses ridin' on a bumble bee,*
> *Settin' de prisoned and de humble free!*' [1]

and, incidentally, burning and pillaging as he

[1] *John Brown's Body*, S. V. Benét.

came, after the time-honoured method of con-
querors. And his 'rascals'

'Having been told to forage, loot as they can
And leave a wound that rankles for sixty years.' [1]

They set fire to Middleton House, and of the
old house, like a bird shot to bits, only a wing
remains. One would have said that the remembrance of its past would have saved it,
even from Sherman's 'rascals.'

. . . .

But the Gardens have survived. Henry
Middleton, of two hundred years ago, worked
his slaves to good purpose. He, like his father,
and most wealthy Carolinians of that time, had
been educated in England, and it was a time
when Horticulture and the making of gardens
was fashionable. Henry Middleton sent to
England for an 'experienced Landscape Gardener' to carry on the work that his father,
Arthur, had begun. He gave the Englishman
a hundred slaves to have and to hold, for
better for worse, to obey his commands as
unhesitatingly as though they were a hundred
wives, and for ten years the English Gardener
worked on the Middleton Gardens. He cannot

[1] *John Brown's Body*, S. V. Benét.

53

have had a wish ungratified. Labour at command, a perfect situation, with river and forest
lending themselves to his intention, and a
climate that would woo any walking stick to
blossom like Aaron's rod.

He used his opportunities well. The Gardens, ringed by the broad stream of the Ashley
river, are as artful as they are artistic. Terraces
that command the ample view of river, and
marsh, and far-reaching plain, with a ruined
cotton mill in the middle distance, as if placed
there for effect. Enormous Camellia Japonica
trees, the first brought to America, gaudy as
Christmas trees, with their formal white and
cherry-coloured rosettes. Shaded walks that
on a sudden reveal a little lovely space of water,
so still that it is hard to say where the reflected
flames of the azaleas end and the flowers themselves begin. The gorgeous collection of azaleas
that William Middleton brought to his gardens
in 1846 is one of the chief glories of the place.
And not the least of the wonders for the ignorant sightseers from Ireland, was the 'Spanish moss,' the extraordinary parasite that has
fastened upon the great Live Oaks, muffling
them (as I have seen, in my own country,

on an early September morning, furze bushes muffled and grey with gossamer webs), blotting their outline against the sky as if with swathes of cotton wool, hanging from their huge branches in grey-green trails that suggest nothing so much as the long whiskers of Early Victorian gentlemen of fashion.

Arthur Middleton, having made his garden, and helped to free his country, built himself a big grey stone tomb among the azaleas and camellias. We came on it suddenly, in a green shade, where

> *'All the flowers and trees do close*
> *To weave the garlands of Repose.'*

One hopes that he was sleeping sound while his countrymen were burning his house.

. . . .

After Middleton Place, the Magnolia Gardens, wonderful as they are, with azaleas everywhere, clad in all the hues of sunset, seemed less memorable. Yet why must comparisons be made where such beauty is in question?

There is one glory of the sun, and another glory of the moon, and why should the greater glory dim the less?

CHAPTER VII

AFTER the Charleston Gardens, Charleston itself, and so far from arriving there, as the song suggests, '*early in de mornin*',' it was late in the afternoon when we drove along the river front and drew up near the Battery, beside one of the Early Georgian 'Colonial' houses, that with their wonderful wrought-iron gates and balconies, and their almost tropical gardens, help to make Charleston the beautiful city that it is.

The lady who had recently, so gallantly, taken on the rôle of Protector of the Poor, now, with a continuing gallantry, introduced us to the owners of this old mansion, and by their great kindness we were privileged to see it all, upstairs and downstairs, with its perfectly proportioned panelled rooms, and contemporary decorations and furniture, looking — as one would imagine — just as it looked two hundred years or so ago, when the ancestors of its present owner saw fit, like Kubla Khan, to decree unto themselves '*a stately pleasure-dome.*'

We drove round the town, and saw from without the famous Pringle House, and from within, St. Michael's Church, an imposing building of the school of Sir Christopher Wren, wherein, on a tablet to General Moultrie, an American soldier of the Revolution, the following tribute to his prowess may be found:

> '*He gave the British their first Defeat,*
> *despite the Sheltered Discipline of Despots.*'

It is a fine phrase, but who or what the Discipline of the Despots sheltered is not explained. For my sister and me, on the other hand, the expression is singularly appropriate. From the moment of our arrival in America we had known nothing save the Sheltering Discipline of Despots, and, humiliating though the admission may be, had thoroughly enjoyed it and thriven under it (unlike the British Forces). Now, reviewing our American adventure, I see a succession of Despots, all equally resolved on sheltering us in such demoralising comfort —

not to say luxury — that had we developed
the conceit, the impudence, and the greed of
two pampered Pekinese, no just person could
have considered the fault was ours.

．　　．　　．　　．　　．　　．　　．　　．

Following on the Gardens and Charleston,
another experience awaited us, fortunate as
we were beyond the common lot of tourists,
since our latest despot had invited us to spend
a couple of days at Dean Hall, a Southern
Plantation of the most authentic type.

Another early Christy Minstrel song had
taught me that

'In South Carolina the Darkies grow,'

and it was entirely in the picture to find that
at Dean Hall, a real Southern house, old and
dignified, with wide pillared verandahs, and
long lofty rooms, in which pictures, books, and
furniture all confirmed the tradition of the
ancient culture of the South, the service was
exclusively 'darky,' home-grown darky, and
'the blacker the better!'

This we were told whenever the subject of
servants was discussed — that subject which
has so terrible an interest for those in the
throes of search, and that can be so boring to

the care-free Bird of Passage. But we, Birds of Passage though we were, found the question of the capabilities of these Children of Ham, whose qualities, such as they are, only appear to develop in servitude, intensely interesting. We had learnt to speak of 'negroes,' or 'coloured people,' or 'darkies,' — it was noticeable that where the most friendly, almost feudal relations existed between white employer and black employed, no one spoke of 'niggers.' Great is the force of habit; those who have begun life with black 'Mammies' and coloured 'House-boys' to minister to them, will not sympathise with the objection raised by one of my friends learned in the classics. She declared that the sight of a black thumb on the edge of her dinner-plate made her think of what Horace said in a similar connection:

'An intense disgust turns the stomach should the servant touch the cup with his greasy hands!'

But this is fantastic hypercriticism. Above and beyond his professional merits (and these are often *hors concours*) the darky servant has a special gift for providing his employer with entertainment, even though this may, some-

59

times, be not unmixed with exasperation. What is the drawback of a black thumb when one remembers Mittie's apology to my sister for having failed to find a missing article — missing, be it said, by no fault of Mittie's:

'I don't like to plunder around too much!' (even as an Irish mason of predatory habit, who, having prowled in a neighbour's yard in vain attempt to abstract a ladder, known by him to exist, excused himself for his failure — 'I wouldn't wish to make too strict a search for it!')

Or again, the letter of a negro poultry-keeper, in whose charge were sixty-five turkeys.

'Dear Mam the turkies ain't doin well turn over.' The owner of the turkeys turned the page as desired and read 'They're all dead.'

Such care to break bad news gently is not common.

Or the coloured groom's delicate warning to a hard-riding mistress, offered during a check in a strenuous woodland hunt.

'Mis' Mary, Mam, yo' done tore yore breeches clear tru' to de meat!'

Therefore it was that we studied 'Porgy' and 'Mamba's Daughters,' and arrived at the

A COLOURED GIRL

conclusion that in the South only negroes speak of 'niggers,' and then only in dislike or contempt — a fine shade that is hard to understand, since the derivation of both is the same. (Which suggests yet another Christy Minstrelism of my youth

'Cæsar and Pompey berry much alike, specially Pompey'!)

.   .   .   .

We had spoken of 'Spirituals,' asking if they had deserted the Negro Quarters for the concert-rooms of civilization. The answer was sufficing, and gave us an unforgettable experience. That evening, after dinner, a dozen or so of the retainers, indoor women, and field-workers, and house-boys, all black as night, led by the Chef, his white overalls and cap of office well becoming his ebony complexion, assembled in the long, shadowy hall, and sang for us Spirituals, the real thing, loud, rough, impassioned, infinitely more impressive, if not more beautiful, than the sophisticated part-song that has been tamed to drawing-room uses. The singing was understood to be given in honour of the two visitors, and we stood in the doorway of the drawing-room, as it were taking the salute, but I think, like true artists, the singers soon forgot their audience. The Chef would begin, setting the key and the tune, and singing the first line in a strong baritone. A woman's piercing voice would respond with a long wailing note, then, gradually, like a storm rising, the rest would join, antiphonally, one end of the line of singers answering the other, voice after voice breaking in, haphazard, like gusts of wind, shouting the theme, while the rest followed, with strange harmonies, and windy crescendos and diminuendos, and broken time, but with unfailing rhythm; to the listeners in the doorway, a perfect ensemble.

.   .   .   .

Comparable with the negro singing, as passionate, as utterly inconceivable, was The Cypress Garden.

I am well aware that to the average person, as to us, the idea of a cypress garden (without capital letters) probably suggests a quiet corner in a country churchyard, with, as the Early Victorian song says —

> '*Cypress and yew, sorrowful trees,*
> *Tears are your dew, sighs are your breeze*' —

tidy, well-trimmed little trees, drooping suitably, not unduly disturbed by the breeze of sighs.

But otherwise indeed was the Cypress Garden of Dean Hall. Space and time are of less significance on a Carolinian plantation than in most places. We had assumed that, as is usual with gardens, this 'garden' was within a five minutes' stroll of the house. It was our first surprise in the affair to discover that it was a matter of a motor. We sped by long winding avenues through belts of wood, and maize-fields, with bending figures of negro-women, who straightened themselves, and smiled, and waved, and called a cheerful morning greeting to their mistress, and by low marshy tracts, thickly grown with slender trees, and starry bushes of pink and white-blossomed dogwood, till at length the avenue degenerated into a mere track, which plunged into a forest, and the motor ceased.

It was explained to us as we walked along a path through the close-growing trees, that in the older time, when South Carolina rice still headed the market, 'Reserves' of water, lakes, in fact, were required to flood the rice-crop when needed. 'There are about

63

two hundred acres of water in the Cypress Garden.'

The statement was let fall, casually. We maintained a discreet silence, wondering, trying to see the connection between two hundred acres of 'Reserve' water and the Cypress Garden. The wood was full of unfamiliar growths, trees, shrubs, and creepers that I knew naught of; but every now and then a pink, or rose, or burning orange bush of azaleas would blossom between the trees, and gorgeous daffodils were everywhere, such daffodils as, of a reasonable size, we knew at home, King Alfred, and Madame de Graaf, and Emperor, and many more, but fed here on the Food of the Gods and grown gigantic.

It was a dull day, without sun, or much light; and it was dark in the wood, but when we reached the Cypress Garden it seemed as though we had wandered out of the world we knew, into a world of dream, and had arrived at some suburb of Hades, at once beautiful and terrible.

A turn in the path had brought us to the shore of what had been 'the Reserve,' an expanse of black, glassy-still water, stretching as far as one could see; and standing in it, growing in it, innumerable multitudes of huge cypress trees, their grey smooth trunks, bare of as much as a twig, reaching up, seventy feet and more, into the roof of darkness that their branches made. The inky water was like a black mirror, darkly repeating the long grey stems, endless ranks of them, going away in dim perspective, stems and reflections, reality and illusion, indistinguishable. An inconceivable place, beautiful and unearthly. One felt as though a handful of that black water would serve as the handful of ink in which the Indian clairvoyant sees fortunes, good and bad, and that the fortune seen in it must foretell tragedy.

The Master of Dean Hall had brought the vision of a landscape-artist to supplement Nature's strange handiwork, and had constructed high, narrow embankments, intersecting the water, with snaky turns and twists, and rough, queer little timber bridges joining the pathways, made from slain companions of the growing trees, whose timber, hard as iron, is said to defy Time and decay.

We walked along the narrow ways for, as it felt, miles; occasional long alleys between the trees intensified the feeling of endlessness, and the conviction that nothing remained of the world we used to know but those dim elephant-grey stems, and the mirroring blackness. Here and there strange growths, a foot or two in height, like clubs, black and lumpy and gnarled, grew out of the water near the bank. These were the dwarfed lungs of the trees, that, in some mysterious way, rose from their roots, and fed them with air.

We went silently, in single file, along the bank, following our guide through this dream-like place as Dante followed Virgil. Conversation does not prosper in Purgatory. Suddenly Virgil paused. Two little dogs had been of our company, and were not now to be seen. Then we heard that an alligator had been seen in these depths only yesterday, and alligators are as fond of dogs as we are — and there might be rattlesnakes about — although, perhaps, it was rather early for rattlesnakes —

It wanted but that... But the little dogs came home with us.

CHAPTER VIII

'A cry more tunable
was never holla'd to, nor cheer'd with horn,'

and yet it was full midnight, and although it was nearly dark when we had arrived at Hickory Nut Gap, I had noted the beautiful skyline of wooded peaks, and it did not suggest a hunting country, except, possibly, for Herne the Hunter, or the Hounds of the Brocken.

I got out of bed and stood at my open window. The furry — or, more properly, firry — outline of the mountain was quite clear against the pale moonlit sky. Below all was dark, and the mournful broken music wandered back and forth, and I thought of Kerry, and of the black and tan hounds crying their hare round and round the valley of Aghatubrid, and of the pack of white hounds, that are heard some-

67

times, at midnight, in the Wood of Annagh, that is in Ross, County Galway (and once were seen, like a white cloud, coming out of the wood, going back to Fairyland, one supposes).

And then I thought that maybe it was dreaming I was, and I not out of bed at all — (because I was very sleepy, and the idiom of Ireland welled up when I thought of the Irish hounds).

But after all I had not been mistaken; we were now among the mountains of North Carolina, and next morning I learned that I had heard the trencher-fed hounds of the farmers who live round about the Gap, and that I should probably hear the same on most of these nights of moonlight.

Then I heard that it was the custom of the hill men of these forest regions to meet at some place high up in the mountains, late, in that darkness wherein, as the psalm says, all the beasts of the forest do creep forth, and then to loose their hounds upon the night, while they make a fire, and sit round it, and gossip, and drink (very appropriately) 'Moonshine,' and listen luxuriously to the striving hounds in the forest depths below and around them.

This way of hunting is, no doubt, very good fun for the hounds, but for the hunters it misses the pleasure that there is in following a trencher-fed pack of 'Kerry Beagles' in the Kerry mountains. Seeing the tall, light-limbed hounds searching the heather and the clumps of bracken, spreading and clustering, feathering on the line, snatching the pride of place from each other, flinging themselves into the chase with but one wild soul among them — I cannot think that gossip and 'moonshine' can make up for the loss of these.

The object of the hunting in these North Carolinian hills is the classic pursuit of the fox, but I was told that the hounds have no regard for the conventions, and will run anything that 'will roar before them' (as was said of a pack in the County Cork, long ago) and who can blame them, with no one to explain to them what constitutes 'riot,' and how scandalous it is to hunt, as one might say, for the pot, and eat jack-rabbits?

There are big wild-cats in these thick-forested mountains, who can show a very formidable front, and it must take stout-hearted hounds to tackle them — big heavy

69

lads, with short tails, terrible in battle. And this also can Hindenburg's Line say of the 'Wildcat Regiment' that was raised in these hills, and was, so we were told, among the first of the conquering troops in that tremendous break-through of the Allies.

The mountaineers of North Carolina are a people apart, of nearly unmixed English descent, who, having toilfully trekked into and taken possession of these high solitudes, took root among the rocks and trekked no more. Cecil Sharpe, the collector of Folksong, (now, unhappily, dead) has told me of how among these Southern mountains, he chanced upon a community of veritable Elizabethans, sixteenth century in talk, and customs, almost in dress. He said that he had found that they danced the dances of Queen Elizabeth's time, but that they had lost the right tunes, and these he was able to teach to them from his store of Folktunes. A curious *vision of the world antique* vouchsafed in the most modern country in the world!

It may be hoped that Cecil Sharpe's trail into that valley, so well lost for so many centuries, has been obliterated, and that these

New World Elizabethans have not now been brought up to date and taught 'cake-walking,' or that most hideous and uncouth of all dances, the 'Charleston'! (One sympathizes with that beautiful city in being made to stand god-mother for so unlovely an exercise!)

Other customs of the mountains are even more strictly Early English than are their dances, and they are certainly less attractive. The obedience exacted by the male gorilla, by force of arms (literally) of his females, is equally incumbent on the wives of the hill farmers. If such was the Elizabethan practice, it becomes comprehensible why Queen Elizabeth remained unmarried, even though Philip of Spain, or even Essex, might not have expected her to darn his socks, and to cook his food, and to await, with the dogs, the remnants left for them when their mutual master had satisfied himself. Such, I was assured, is the custom of the mountains. I have heard also of a mountaineer who had what may be called a trekking complex, and as soon as he had cleared a space of virgin forest and made a dwelling-place on it, would become restless and dissatisfied, and the sale of the home she

had just made habitable, would be the first
intimation to his wife that she had to 'pull out
on the long trail' again.

   .   .   .   .

The mountaineers, like other primitives,
possess a special *flair* for funerals. (In Ireland,
for example, I have been told of a cook who
stipulated with a new employer that she should
be permitted to go to 'Public Amusements,
Circuses, and Funerals, and the like o' that.')
Nothing in North Carolina in the life of a
relative 'becomes him like the leaving of it,'
and all expenditure on his behalf is strictly
posthumous.

An old woman of the mountains died. An
old, old creature, one of these survivals of
a past age, who looked as though she might
have confirmed or discredited the Elizabethan
legend from personal experience. Her son, who
had waited many years for the opportunity,
determined on giving a funeral — as it were
a function, like a public dinner — in her
honour. He was a stern, silent old farmer, very
old, very poor, yet resolved on spending all the
savings of his long, hard life, one hundred and
seventy dollars, on launching his mother with

a splendour that would ensure her reception into the best society in the next world.

The burying-place was on the crest of a mountain, and as the procession, gorgeously plumed, and weepered and craped, crawled up the height, a terrific storm broke. Rain fell in torrents, thunder roared, and lightning blazed. In the thick of the storm the graveyard was reached, and there the ghastly custom of opening the coffin for a last farewell was complied with. And thereupon, the grim, and ordinarily speechless old son, flung himself across the open coffin, weeping as wildly as the skies, howling to the dead old woman assurances of eternal devotion, at full stretch of his lungs, while the thunder rolled and banged from mountain to mountain, and the lightning's harsh and crooked flashes played about the coffin, like the fire from heaven that blazed on Elijah's altar on Mount Carmel.

.   .   .   .

Spring in North Carolina is quite an undertaking. There is so much to be done that Flora has her hands full. So many hill-meadows to decorate, and shrubs — Kalmia and Dogwood, in the mountains, keeping the pine trees' feet

warm — to be spangled; and fruit-trees everywhere, to be taught to dodge early frosts and
to remember that beauty isn't everything.
She was only just beginning to get busy when
we arrived, and the common lot of sight-seers,
in selecting the moment when things were not
quite looking their best, was, of course, ours.
Nevertheless, the sunrise-pink of the peach
blossom did not fail us, and the Forsythia,
which might well be accepted as the national
flower of America, was in full glory.

My wanderings in these early months of
spring, took me from Aiken to Boston, with
sundry midway divergences, and the pure,
canary-yellow clouds of blossom ran up the
long rail-journeys with me, going north always,
leaving summer behind, and finding spring
ever a little way ahead. The apple-trees up at
Hickory Nut Gap had barely begun to show
colour, and the Kalmias' robes of dark green
gave no sign of what they meant to do later on,
but the Dogwood, (which is quite unlike what
we call dogwood) was full of lovely flower, its
white and pink discs conspicuous against the
dark background of Mountain Laurel (which
we know as Kalmia) and pine trees.

There came a day straight from heaven, when it was proposed to motor the visitors to the top of Mount Mitchell. It sounded ambitious, and some feminine doubts were expressed. Mount Mitchell is the highest mountain in the Appalachian system, if not — if we may trust North Carolinian estimates — in the world, and it was a long way off.

But since to express a doubt of a car's capacity is to crystallise its owner's determination to prove it (as a poet has said, '*To wound is but to harden*') — it needed but this to elicit an order to mobilise the luncheon baskets.

Our way lay through Asheville, and thereafter, through a green and lovely valley, we were borne swiftly — (very swiftly, our host, who was at the wheel, being of those who do not hold with the advice to make haste slowly) — to the point at which the admirable cement-laid road changes its character and becomes a packet of precipitous hairpins, facing upwards towards Mount Mitchell.

Our leader, with an intrepidity that some of us found excessive, addressed his car to the hairpins. The way was narrow, a wall of rock on the one hand, on the other a fathomless

75

abyss. We sped upwards at some forty m.p.h., cutting corners with a skilled precision that left but a blade or two of grass between us and eternity, until, at a bridge across a ravine, a halt was called to water the car.

Its occupants, six in number, alighted, not without gratitude for the moment of respite, and when the word was again Excelsior, two of the party, whose complexions had noticeably faded during the ascent, announced that they would prefer to stay at the point now attained to, and enjoy such view as it offered, while the car proceeded to the summit. It was explained to them that the further ascent of the car would probably involve for them a long and tedious delay, as it was still twenty-five miles to the summit.

'Even so ——' they replied, with firmness.

Here, however, the Guardian Angel of those with weak heads interposed. It was found that the car was running a temperature (or its equivalent in cars) and was 'boiling.' The gradients of the coming five-and-twenty miles would become more acute, and streams less frequent. An alternative scheme was propounded, and the big car slid down the hairpins as sweetly as if she were gliding in a stream of oil.

It is well, when possible, to slur over defeat, and there was consolation in the reflection that views from mountain-tops have little more than geographical interest — like photographs taken from airplanes — there is one aspect only, and the only beauty left is that of colour. This is, I believe, heresy, so let me hurry on to the Valley of the Rocky Broad River, whose beauty was sufficient solace, had solace been required. And to Lake Lure, that amazing achievement, that is the imperishable memory of a dream, one man's dream.

For Irish people it will be enough to say that the Upper Lake of Killarney came immediately to the minds of two Irish wanderers, and left them incapable of finding a word of higher praise.

We heard how a vision came to a dreamer, who was also a man of action. How he bought the wide space between the mountains, and dammed the river that ran through the valley — a valley ten miles long, that ends in a neck narrow enough to make the dreamed-of lake a reality. The life of the long valley was

77

gradually drowned. Villages and churches, slowly vanishing, to be lost for ever, like the Round Towers of other days that are hidden under the waters of Lough Neagh. Only those who — one would fancy — would care least — would, perhaps, laugh at so much trouble being taken for what had become valueless to them — were considered. The stipulation was made that before the valley was submerged, the contents of the graveyards were to be moved to higher ground.

CHAPTER IX

THE spring had fairly come before we left the mountains of North Carolina. Now, in Irish midwinter, when I think of that beautiful country, I seem to see it simmering in sunshine, with drifts of peach blossom pink, and forsythia gold, and the pale, delicious green of young leaves, set against that sombre background of incessant fir forests.

Washington, in March, at 7 A.M., wore a different complexion, (and so, indeed, did we — mauve, with pink accents) and we may be excused for having mistaken the sparse opening buds on the long avenue of Japanese cherry-trees, for a dash of snow.

We did no more than change trains there, and pushed on to our destination in the heart of the best hunting country in Virginia. The season was just at an end, and we were lucky in arriving in time to see the last meet of one of the many packs of foxhounds that in Virginia carry on the sporting tradition of three hundred or so of years.

A Ford car does not pretend to get to hounds with the determination and agility of an Aiken buggy, but it can deal with the back roads of Virginia with a masterly vigour that would inspire confidence even in those whose nerves had not been braced by the drastic experiences of Aiken. That this privilege had been ours has already been recorded, and more than once that day, as the Ford careered along a rudimentary by-road, it stood us in good stead. It is unbecoming in a visitor to make comparisons; I will therefore only venture the suggestion that as between an Aiken forest-track, and a Virginian back road, it is a matter of fifty-fifty, and will leave it at that.

The meet was a small one, not above twenty riders, and again, as at Aiken, the high quality of the horses was very striking and impressive. I had noted — when able to withdraw my eyes from the perils of the road — many solid Irish-looking walls, that, with the strong tim-

ber 'snake-fences,' make the country a suffi-
ciently stiff proposition from the riders' point
of view. It was interesting to see that several
of the horses were much of the type of Irish
three-quarter-bred hunters, and I recall one
handsome big bay weight carrier — (who was
carrying our hostess, and could very easily
have carried two more like her) — who would
have held his own in the best company in any
Irish Hunt.

But the hounds ——?

I suppose if, stamped on the retina, to reign
there, apart, unspotted from the world, there
is a definite and well-marked ideal, it is impossible to bring an unbiassed mind to a wholly
different type of anything. And this applies,
supremely, to hounds. So I will offer no opinion on these — to me — so strange and unfamiliar red and yellow creatures, beyond a dif-
fident suggestion that if a red Irish setter were
neatly shaved, and the permanent wave obliterated, he might — but, perhaps, it is better
to remember the saying that 'There are some
things too serious for joking, and one of them's
potatoes.' So it is also with hounds.

· · · · · · · · · ·

81

An early fall of snow, a very cold wind, and a fair share of rain, had not encouraged the foxes to stay above ground, and I learned that it was not customary in this country to stop the earths. (A departure from the usual practice, which shows a confidence in the gentlemanly feeling of foxes, and their wish to show sport, that would certainly be abused in Ireland.)

A couple of long tracts of woodland were the first draw. False alarms, (which is usually another name for rabbits) kept us, degraded roadsters in the Ford, rushing up and down a steep and deeply-rutted track through the wood, stimulated by brief glimpses of the riders, as well as by the crescendo and diminuendo of distant hound-music. Finally, by a fresh series of bohireens (which is the Irish for a little road, and usually implies a bad one), we bumped home, the undaunted Ford making nothing of difficulties that might have given pause even to a buggy, and we had no sooner entered upon lunch, than the cry of hounds lifted us from our seats, and by rushing from the table with mannerless haste, we were in time to see the pack go by, in full cry, and

UP HILL AT A 'CHICKEN-COOP'

red and yellow though they be, the cry was of the authentic classic music.

They swept on up a long and steep pasture field; we, faint but pursuing, longed for the Ford, but even on our own inadequate legs, were in time to see the Field jumping a 'chicken-coop,' which is the pet name for a contrivance that looks like the roof of a little buried house, and, fixed astride a wire fence, cheats it of its powers of mischief. From the top of the hill we watched the hunt across a ploughed field, its orange-coloured clay seeming to swallow the orange-coloured pack, as a heather-dark mountain side will swallow the black Kerry hounds. On the farther side of the plough they jumped a wall, a good honest stone wall; it brought to me a memory of days in East Galway with the 'Blazers,' as I watched the riders widen out and gallop at it with a fine freedom, each where he or she liked.

After that we saw them fade into specks in the distance of the vast stretch of open fertile country that goes away to the Blue Mountains. We heard next day that they had run for an hour and forty minutes, and had killed their fox. A great performance on such a day of chill wind, with rain and snow overhead.

CHAPTER X

BEFORE we left Ireland any talk of our coming visit to the United States was certain to provoke comments on the solemn subject of Prohibition, that were sometimes serious, sometimes, and more often, facetious, taking the form of superfluous condolences on what were assumed to be our coming sufferings. Travellers had told moving tales of the hardships that the Volstead Act had involved, which seemed rather at variance with the companion assurances that every citizen of the States went to bed blind drunk.

But in our experience the singular fact emerged that in the British Isles the much-debated Act had seemed a far more vital affair than it appeared to be in its native land, and for very superficial strangers it was difficult to resist the impression that what is called The Liberty of the Subject had not been very seriously interfered with. Save in a few households that honourably respected the Law, and, having the courage of their opinions, obeyed it, we found that Prohibition was regarded as a Counsel of Perfection, and was treated as such counsels are wont to be served. In fact it may be admitted that, in spite of the 'dry' laws, but few of the dinner-parties to which we were hospitably invited failed of that trusty nourisher — (or may one say 'wet' nurse?) — of conversation, champagne.

Cocktails, in all their many and morbid mixtures, were equally unfailing. For my part, being unable to appreciate their complicated appeal, I can take no credit to myself for obedience to the law. Had I, indeed, accepted all that were proffered to me — sometimes, as at one hospitable Country-Club, four deep — I should soon have been eligible for deportation as a thoroughly Undesirable Alien! After all, it is more incumbent on guests to observe their host's family regulations than it is on the children of the house.

85

At home one has heard so much of the habitual intoxication of the Best People in the States, that it was not without a slight feeling of having been cheated of a sensation, that, at our first dinner party, we did not find ourselves rising from the table and leaving our fellow guests under it. As a matter of fact but one case in point came my way. The occasion was a smart wedding, at which floods of champagne had insured that the healths of the bride and bridegroom should be thoroughly established.

During that always age-long interval, when the Bride has vanished, like the sun behind clouds, to reappear in renewed splendour, I found myself seated between two gentlemen, unknown to me, who were rather obviously Anti-Prohibitionists. Difficult though they must have found it, they were resolved to be agreeable. One law-breaker talked dreamily, and at great length, of the prospects of the corn crop in the Middle West; the other, with brief intervals of what seemed like sleep, imparted to me, fitfully, the details of a recent base-ball match (a game which I have yet to see, and never expect to understand). Duller

86

boon companions I have never met. I would not borrow a shilling to get drunk with either of them.

. . . .

In our experience American agreeability needs no spur. At one of the gayest and most brilliant of our entertainments iced water 'set the table on a roar' with such success that — as can happen at an equally matched tug-of-war — deadlock ensued, and what can only be called a deafening silence was the result. I have seen, I cannot say heard, London bus-conductors carry on, amidst the thunder of traffic, a conversation that was quite inaudible to the uninitiated. Thus, I suppose, the screams of our fellow-guests, all being agreeable at the full stretch of their lungs, were mutually apprehended, while I, unable to intercept so much as a word, could only respond with ineffectual, and I am sure, perfectly irrelevant yells. But it is a fault — if indeed a fault it be — on the right side. It is only the defect of its qualities; to the ear of the hostess the yells are music.

. . . .

These divagations have led me far from Virginia, and Virginia is decidedly a place to return to, in memory, if no more material form of travel is possible.

We were in Virginia, and it was the first week in April; the weather was cold and unseasonable, and we were wondering what had happened to Spring, when there came a week that was like a pioneer sent by Summer to blaze a path for her. Blaze is in truth the right word. The temperature, in a single night, shot up to over 90°, and the sun, that we thought we had seen the last of at Aiken, began to make apologies for past neglect that were rather excessive in their fervour.

But although 90° in the shade is undoubtedly a high temperature, so much depends on where the shade is found. At the Puppy Show of the Middelburg Hunt, seated on a lawn in the young green shade of tall trees, devouring an admirable lunch, in no less excellent company, we found no fault with the sun.

We were, unfortunately, rather late in arriving, and only two or three couples remained to be judged. The judging ring — as is usual on these nerve-wracking occasions — was surrounded by the anxious 'walkers,' those indispensable mainstays of any hunt, priceless beyond rubies, whose joys and sorrows culminate at this supreme moment. The glory of delivering to the Master a creditable well-walked puppy, possibly a Prizewinner, being dimmed by the thought of the parting with the loved and cherished Dulcet and Dimity, in whose frightened eyes is already foreknowledge of doom. The mind — and I speak as one who has many times suffered — should then be firmly turned towards those bone-cemeteries in the flower-garden, those other boots, whose gnawed remains are found on the tennis-lawn, those chickens, slain in their prime — But even so...

With hearts full of sympathy for all concerned, we squeezed our way into the front row. There is no more beautifully-proportioned creature than a good foxhound, and these puppies were no less charming than they are wont to be. We learned that they were crossbred between imported and native foxhounds, and we saw enough of the entry to realise that an English and American alliance is, as one might expect, productive of a high standard of quality!

.   .   .   .

The popularity of Foxhunting, and the deep and general interest that is taken in it (and this, as I found later, not only in Virginia) was one of the surprises that America had for me. Enthusiasts were many, and the cult of Horse and Hound provides an unfailing point of contact, and a subject for conversation that is ˙ as engrossing as it is inexhaustible. (So I have heard it said, not without acrimony, by those who do not hunt.)

There were not, I think, many such at this gathering. An immense marquee held some four hundred farmers, staunch supporters of hunting, and on the lawn, under the trees, we met riders from many hunts, as well as many of our friends from Aiken, who had made the long journey from the South, with the remarkable indifference to the effort of travel, by rail and by night, that was another of our American surprises.

After the Puppy show and lunch, an enormous fleet of motor-cars was mysteriously mobilised from some remote and necessarily vast parking-place, to convey the multitude to the Hunt Point-to-Point Races. It is yet another of the American surprises that the automobile has entirely supplanted not only the harness-horse and the bicycle, but also the walking-stick! No one walks. I am sure that no self-respecting American ghost would now walk. Every workman appears to possess a car, and motors to his job. I have commented upon the elegance of a car in the garage of a friend, and been told that it belonged to her cook, a negro lady, who would no doubt decline to join in the 'Spiritual' that requests a sweet chariot to swing low, unless she were assured of its being a Lincoln Saloon. The universal possession of cars is said to be one of the many arguments in favour of Prohibition, and when I saw the road to the Races packed, wheel to wheel, with cars, I realised what might have been the result had their drivers been drinking the Toasts proper to a Hunt-Luncheon in the old-fashioned way!

. . . .

Thanks to a very efficient and determined chauffeur we found ourselves viewing the races from a position that approximated to the Royal

Enclosure at Ascot. In order to arrive at it we had left the road, and pushed our way across the level field behind the starting-place of the course, and had climbed a steep hill, and pierced the heart of a pine-wood. When, at last, the car could by no possibility go any farther, and the old-fashioned expedient of walking was forced upon us, we found ourselves, in a very few yards, at the edge of the wood, and on the brow of a hill from which nearly the whole course was visible.

A little below where we had seated ourselves on the warm grass, was the Judge's box, a front seat on the top of a Four-in-hand. A beautiful grassy stretch of rolling country lay below us. The jumps, as far as we could see them, were of timber, high and stiff, and the course, which must have been something over two miles in length, had to be taken twice round (a heartbreaking feature of so many courses). I do not propose to attempt a description of the racing, interesting and often exciting though it was, for several reasons, of which I think one will suffice — that I have forgotten the names of both horses and riders.

But one horse I have not forgotten, nor his

name, 'Silvercrest,' even though he had nothing more important to do than canter about the course, carrying one of the stewards, who was his owner. For Silvercrest is a horse to be remembered, a creature memorable alike for his achievements and his beauty, a type on which to 'make one's eye.' He was not a big horse; hardly, I should say, — thinking of what he felt like when I stood beside him — sixteen hands, and so perfectly balanced as to appear less than that. His colour is grey, a very silvery grey, because, in the sole respect of colour, Time has touched him. I had seen him from far off, and had asked for the honour of an introduction, and my hostess, who knew every horse there that was worth knowing, as well as their riders, kindly performed the ceremony. Silvercrest stood still while I spoke to him, regarding me with a dark and lovely eye that was so full of wisdom as to bring assurances of the possibility of all the wonder stories of the wonder pony 'Black Bear'; (of whom one of his interviewers told me that the more you knew of him the more convinced you were that you had gone out of your mind). I heard that Silvercrest had won every jumping competi-

93

tion for which he had been entered (in the States I found the rational rule obtained that all Hunter Competitions involve jumping). In his day nothing could beat him; all the greatest prizes that America has to give were his. His judgment of pace, length, and height, was said to be faultless; he was incapable of making a mistake; in fact he was so incredibly, so overwhelmingly perfect a being that the inevitable human desire to show intelligence by fault-finding, endeavoured to assert itself.

In a mental whisper I asked myself, '*Has he quite bone enough?*' (I try to indicate a whisper by italics — in face of his record, one criticised, even in thought, in a whisper)... I am reminded of a game of Bridge, in the course of which my sister brought off a Grand Slam. As the last triumphant trick was gathered in, her partner solemnly reproved her for what he considered to be an error in the playing of the hand. But what more did he want?... Unquestionably Silvercrest has enough bone!

· · · · · · · · ·

I was told a story by a young lady, a lady of Virginia, who was bred in its traditions, and was born of a family that for generations had

94

helped to make its history. The story was told
delightfully, and it seems to me so romantic in
all its implications, that I hope I may be forgiven for trying, however lamely, to retell it
here.

It begins some seventy years ago, not long
before the outbreak of the Civil War, when the
grandfather of the narrator, head of a great
family, owner of a great estate, Master, Law-
giver, almost Life-arbiter of the unnumbered
company of slaves that cultivated his land,
and were his to have and to hold till death did
them part, was still the lawful proprietor of his
lawful possessions.

The Master, like most Virginian gentlemen,
was a lover of horses. He considered that the
quality of the horses of his native county,
might, with advantage, be improved, and he
sent to England and bought there a thorough-
bred stallion, and brought him to Virginia.
After a time the Master decided to lend to
a friend the horse, whose charming name was
Ambercrest — (he was possibly the ancestor of
Silvercrest, but I know not if this be so). The
friend lived far off, at the other side of the
great county of Virginia, but in those days,

though distances were greater, time was of less importance than now. The Master put Ambercrest in charge of an old slave, named Garner, and sent the pair off together, to walk several hundred miles to the stables of his friend.

I have been told, and have myself seen, how soothing and sensible negro grooms can be in their handling of horses, and I have no doubt but that old Garner and young Ambercrest were good friends, and that they set forth on their long journey together in peace and amity.

But they never reached the stables for which they were bound. The terrible war between North and South began. The Master went away to fight, and for four years he fought for the rights of the South. And fought in vain. When, at last, he came home again, he summoned the creatures who had been his slaves, and told them that they were free, and could go when and where they liked, but that those who cared to stay in their old quarters could do so, and they would be kept and cared for until they died, as was the habit of his family with their slaves (and was, I imagine, the habit of most of the old Virginian gentlepeople, and not the exception, 'Uncle Tom's Cabin'

96

and Mrs. Beecher Stowe notwithstanding!)
I gathered that many of the newly-freed
stayed, and the Master and his family took up
their lives again, and made the best they could
out of what was left to them. But no word
came of Ambercrest, the English horse, and
Garner, the old slave.

There came a day in the sunny Southern
spring when the Master and the Mistress and
their children were sitting on the lawn in
front of the house. They could see down the
avenue, and coming quietly towards them between the flowering shrubs, they perceived
a large speck and a small one. The Master
stood up and stared hard at them.

'By God!' he said, 'here are Ambercrest and
Garner!'

And so it was. They had never reached their
destination, for the war was upon them long
before they had gone half way, and all was
chaos and red ruin in that much fought-over
country. What, precisely, Garner did with
his charge is not known. Only that he vowed
the Yankee soldiers should never get him. He
seems to have found some building approxi-
mating to a stable, and — as we say in Ireland

— 'put him to hide' there. He worked to keep the horse fed, and every night he slept in the hiding-place beside Ambercrest, with an open knife under his hand, so that if the Yankees came, and found the horse, he might hamstring him to save him from captivity.

CHAPTER XI

I AM NOT a good sight-seer. In fact, I may say, definitely, that I am a bad one. Certainly I fall very short of the standard set by an acquaintance, an American lady, whom I met at Aix-les-Bains. She told me that she and her daughters had ascended all the principal church and other towers in Europe.

It did not surprise me that following on these achievements she had been ordered the most intensive treatment that Aix has to offer. Deep massage of what she called her limbs was a leading feature of what she was now compelled to endure. She said that the only thing that made these ascents tolerable was that on attaining the summit she shut her eyes, and so remained until set by a daughter on the top step of the spiral descent.

'I certainly would have been a Jump to Glory Jane if I had looked out over those parapets,' she remarked; 'I never was meant for a steeple-jack.'

This seemed probable. I agreed, and I told her of a steeple-jack who was doing some repairs to the topmost spire of Cork Cathedral. He had observed two little girls, on the ground far below him, who had been standing there for a considerable time. Sound rises, and he heard one say to the other: 'Come on, Bridgie, come on! There's no good staying here!'

The other replied: 'Ah, hold on a while, Katie, he might fall yet!'

The steeple-jack disappointed them, and he told this to the Bishop, and the Bishop told it to me, so this is a true story.

There are however, with regard to the effort of sight-seeing, many less strenuous forms of approaching the task than that inflicted on my American friend. I can confidently recommend the method adopted by our host in Virginia for showing us Washington.

Having been fortified at a palatial hotel, with

a luncheon of the kind that predisposes to contemplation rather than activity, we found that our sight-seeing was to be effected with the minimum of exertion and the maximum of comfort. In a large car we glided round the beautiful city; up and down the leafy avenues with their ordered phalanxes of forest trees (and to each avenue a different variety;) round and about the public buildings, awed by their magnificence, thankful that there was no necessity to visit their roofs by spiral stairs or even by lifts (or should I say elevators?)

A few paramount memories remain with me. One, the splendour of the Lincoln Memorial, with that tremendous, thoughtful figure, seated in the great hall, brooding over the city that had seen his triumph and his death. And the outlook from its doorway, to where, beyond the long stretches of shining water, George Washington's white obelisk 'points to the skies.'

Another memory, an experience in which we were more actively involved, was a visit to the crypts of the new cathedral that is to add to the glories of Washington. At the time of our visit, which was April, 1929, there was very little to be seen above ground, and we, in company with our host and hostess, as well as of a considerable crowd of other sight-seers, were shepherded underground by lay guides — vergers in embryo, presumably — through the labyrinthine passages, crypts, and cellars proper to an orthodox cathedral. My sister and I, being untrained and ill-regulated tourists, strayed from the flock, and it was in a sort of subterranean chapel that we suddenly realised that we were bereft of all human companionship. We attempted to find the way by which we had come, but only succeeded in circumnavigating the chapel and entering it by another doorway. Like two church mice, lost, (and of unusual size,) we scurried along narrow passages, served by occasional electric lights, and found each passage led only to an impassable barricade of timber. I began to remember the mediæval belief that to every church there must be a victim, to insure its stability, who was known by the sinister title of the Church-Grim. Had we been Fate-led to dedicate ourselves to be the Church-Grims of Washington Cathedral? For a few agitated moments it seemed probable, but a fortunate change of direction revealed, far ahead of us, a space of blue daylight. Dismissing the prospect of dedication as Church-Grims, we hurried to the light, and found ourselves in the open air. Close to where we had emerged was a small building in which the flock of which we had formed part was studying a marvellously perfect plaster model of the coming cathedral. And there also, awaiting us, calm, but not, I think, entirely free from anxiety, were our lost protectors.

CHAPTER XII

I HAVE read a book of stories of Kerry — The Kingdom of Kerry, in the Province of Munster, Ireland — and in it there is a story of a young Kerryman, whose name was Foxy John. He had a horse, a fairy horse, which is described as a slender brown horse, and it was given to him by a fairy cowboy. The story goes on to say that:

'Foxy John boasted of the horse that it could 'jump three glens in a pounce, or slip seven moun-'tains in a jump.

'"I will not doubt the leap of your horse," said 'a fair man standing by the shore of a lake, who 'saluted him with the modest and witty expressions 'in vogue at that time, "but," says he, "you can-'"not jump over this lake to fetch me my wife, '"whose hair is as amber, and who is lamenting '"and hanging on to the limb of a tree beyond?"

'Foxy John urged the slender horse with the
'palm of his hand, and he leapt the lake with the
'neatness of a child crossing a stream, and it the
'width of its bare foot. He found the fair man's
'wife, lamenting and hanging on to the limb of a
'tree, and lifting her on his saddle he made one
'pounce back.'

The book in which this story is told is called
'Mary of the Winds,'[1] and it has many other
equally true Kerry stories in it. They were
collected and written down by my friend,
'Enedeen,' and, as she is a woman of Kerry,
I am sure they must be true.

The reason I have remembered Foxy John's
slender brown horse now, is because, on a fine
day in April, we, also, jumped three glens in
a pounce, and if we didn't altogether slip seven
mountains in a jump, we certainly crossed six
mountain ranges in a day's journey; that is to
say, three going, and three returning, which is
the way such things would be reckoned in
Kerry (of whose stories it may sometimes be
said that the less contains the greater, and
a little goes a long way).

[1] *Mary of the Winds and Other Tales*, by Enedeen. (Pub-
lished by John Murray, London.)

As well as the mountain ranges we crossed, on that day's journey, a river whose name — I think I may venture to say — is better known with us in the British Isles than that of any other river the United States can offer. Once on a time its name went round the world, winged by a haunting tune, shouted in sailing ships by sailor-men who, most probably, knew no more of the Shenandoah than that it was a long, melancholy word, which lent itself to the infinitely melancholy tune that set the measure for them as they tramped round with the capstan-bars.

> '*O Shenandoah, I'm bound to leave you,*
>   *Away, you rolling river!*
> *O Shenandoah, I'll not deceive you,*
>   *Away I'm bound to go,*
> *'cross the wide Missouri!*'

Thus the sailors sang, stamping round. One wonders if they — who made it — realised the ineffable fitness of the tune to the words, the poignancy of both?

The days of the sailing ships have passed, and the old shanty, with many of its brethren, has been collected, and civilised, and harmonised, and has been turned loose in drawing-rooms, to be sung with a melting sweetness to which it was quite unaccustomed. Like the sailing ships themselves, who decorate lamp-shades, while their effigies in silver collect dust on side-tables, it has become idle and effete, and no longer inspires men to effort more violent than that of encoring it at an amateur concert.

. . . .

When we heard that — in addition to pouncing three glens and slipping six mountains — we were to cross this river, so well-loved, so widely hymned, we felt suitably excited. But I am not sure that it is advisable to 'see Shelley plain,' and, in matter-of-fact day-light, to visit a place that fancy has made her own. We found the Shenandoah very much like any other river, with no special features, meandering through a pastoral landscape. It does not even reach the sea.

And so the vision of the stately merchant-man, with all her many sails set, dropping down a wide tidal river into the sunset, must be for ever renounced.

. . . .

We were bound for the celebrated Caves of

Luray, whose 'marvellous display of limestone formations' (I quote the Encyclopædia Britannica) 'is considered to exceed that of any other cavern known.' Our way lay through the Shenandoah Valley. A beautiful valley, peaceful and prosperous again, now that nearly seventy years have given it time to forget what History calls the Shenandoah Campaigns. That terrible time when two great armies, whose soldiers spoke the same language, and came of the same stock, and owned the same traditions, raged and fought up and down the long valley, leaving it filled with dark memories of suffering and death.

Slowly we climbed by long zigzags to the top of a high pass, and there paused awhile to look back into the depths from which we had risen. In front, radiant in all the lovely colours of spring, lay the fair valley, of which General Sheridan had said that he had 'destroyed everything that was eatable south of Winchester.'

A thorough, and eminently satisfactory job.

.   .   .   .

'*O Shenandoah! I'm bound to leave you!*'

The inveterate tune came with me as we

sailed away, down the other side of the mountain, and presently found ourselves in what, I suppose, should be called the township of Luray. I do not know what is meant precisely by a township, but it is impossible to describe as a town those entirely unrelated bungalows, villas, and stores, speckled about in what seems an intentional disregard of unity. The entrance to the Caves is concealed in a solid and well-proportioned building, in which all the necessary accessories to sight-seeing are provided — souvenirs, Guides, human and printed, and picture-postcards innumerable, both small and great. Equipped with a very considerate and intelligent elderly guide, as well as with one of the many well-illustrated pamphlets, we were ushered to a small doorway, and found ourselves standing at the head of a long flight of cement steps, looking down into what is called the Grand Vestibule, and realising instantly that even in this, the Cavern's mere antechamber, the marvels transcended anything that we could have thought possible.

. . . .

Not for a moment need it be feared that I propose to attempt, for my own part, to describe the Caves. But I cannot refrain from quotation from the interesting pamphlet with which I provided myself. Even as a literary effort alone it is worthy of high respect, and I trust that by omitting (as far as a sense of honour will permit) inverted commas, I may be credited with some of the glowing phrases that I have culled from it.

. . . .

'Entering the Grand Vestibule, the first emotion felt by the visitor is one of mute wonder.' Thus my instructive pamphlet laid down the position, adding, that possessed by awe and reverence, the visitor should stand amazed in the Royal Chamber of the King of Nature.

Muteness was not the distinguishing feature of any of our party, but we registered the other emotions without difficulty. With sufficient attention to the invaluable pamphlet no one could be at a loss for an emotion, an adjective, or a phrase throbbing with sensibility. We studied it gratefully, and having stood amazed, as directed, we proceeded along cement walks, with stairways, bridges, and iron railings, 'where such were necessary to see all the wonders in the most comfortable manner.' 'Glittering stalactites blaze in front, fluted columns, draperies, in broad folds and a thousand tints, cascades of snow-white stone (illuminated by the electric light) fill the mind with curious sensations of wonder and admiration.'

The panegyrics are not excessive, and they are in keeping with the rich poetic fancy that has inspired the names of the various sections and features of the Caves. What can be more romantic than designations such as Oberon's Grot, Dream Lake, Sacred River, Helen's Scarf? Or, in sterner vein, Giants' Hall, The Swords of the Titans, and Pluto's Chasm? Others there are, such as Bootjack Alley, Lost Blanket, Fishmarket, and Scaly Column, that strike a more prosaic note; but with these the author of my pamphlet does not concern himself, and I prefer to follow his guidance (though it cannot be denied that, in one of the many caverns, where one is shown a long row of tapering stalactites, like herrings hanging by their snouts on a string, 'Fishmarket' fits the facts with singular aptitude).

'Heroic forms,' he tells us, 'loom up on every side, guarding the marvellous beauty of Ti-

111

tania's Veil, and watching over the crystal waters of Diana's Bath. The Elfin Ramble, nearly four hundred feet long by one hundred and twenty-five feet in breadth, is the play-ground of the Princesses of the Fairy Realm. ...' Murmuring these observations to each other, we followed our guide along the 'bewil-dering windings and labyrinthine meanderings through which the tourist must tread his way,' and trod, for upwards of a mile and a half, through one cavern full of fantastic freaks of limestone, after another; through Hades, through the Saracen's Tent, and through the Bridal Chamber. These, we are told, 'bear a striking resemblance to the objects for which we are named,' but this I am unable to corrob-orate from experience. I can, however, testify to the authenticity of the Grand Organ in the Cathedral, a very marvellous formation of tall stalactites that stand, close side by side, and form the pipes of the organ. Our guide pro-duced a little hammer, shod with rubber, and, as a boy rattles a stick along an iron railing, he swept his hammer along the pipes, bringing forth such a wild and tangled rush of music as might stimulate the maddest moment of

112

a Russian Ballet. The tone was beautifully clear, hard, and sweet, and cold, too, as if the sound were struck from tubes of ice. The Guide ended his display with three pure and distinct notes, A, G, F, in as perfect relation to each other as the notes of a piano.

He paused to receive our admiration, and was thus quite unprepared to avert or resist the rape of his hammer. My sister, suddenly, with a swift and masterful snatch, possessed herself of it, and before the startled guide had time to protest, she had hammered a slightly abridged version of 'Rousseau's Dream' out of what the Smithsonian Institution's Report has briefly and mellifluously summarised as 'The Stalactitic and Stalagmitic Ornamentation of Luray.'

(I cannot answer for the correctness of the key, but this is what she played.)

CHAPTER XIII

ONE last memory of Virginia I must not omit from these casual and quite inadequate records.

It began with a luncheon at a Hunt Club with one of the joint Masters of a very well-known pack of 'American' Foxhounds. A charming house, full of pictures of hounds and horses and riders, and a host and hostess versed in sport, and delightfully ready to talk of hunting in the County Cork, from the point of view of personal experience.

It was refreshing to meet riders whose knowledge of Irish hunting had not been gained exclusively with the County Meath Hounds — ('Royal Meath,' though indisputably it is, a great country, and great hunting.) For Munster people however it was impossible to refrain from suggesting that there were Southern hunts which were equally worthy of

IN THE WEST CARBERY KENNELS

recognition by American riders, and we had not been long in the States before the time came when the inevitable mention of Bective — which would seem to be the Mecca of devout American foxhunters — was equivalent to treading on the tail of a Munster coat!

Therefore it was that mutual reminiscences of the Uniteds and the Duhallows, and of County Cork banks, and County Galway walls, were as Songs of Zion in a strange land, and we all set forth after lunch to view kennels and stables, in a mood of what can only be described as sunny repletion.

Interesting to enthusiasts as are hounds and horses and all that pertains to them, it may be possible to say too much about them. Therefore I will silently remember the Orange County 'American' hounds, and the thoroughbred hunters of one of the joint-masters (beautiful horses, looking as fit at this, the end of a hard season, as if the opening meet was to happen next day).

After these things, we had tea in what we were told had been, in the brave days of old, part of the negro quarters of the estate. It was a long low building that had been transformed into a sort of summer house or dolls' house, a caprice that played at being a humble cottage, with every luxury of civilisation concealed beneath a specious rustic simplicity — (which is, to be sure, the perfection of such a 'folly').

We sat at a long, frankly kitchen table, with incongruously dainty fine linen and lace mats (that seem to be one of the peculiar products of the States) under our cups and plates. The chairs were of the plainest; the kettle was boiled in a tiny adjoining scullery, and the scones came out of the oven behind us, 'roaring hot,' as scones should be. We were a crowd of fifteen or twenty people, and how the supply held out was a triumph of prevision and provision. Everyone ate hot scones unrestrainedly and enormously, and talked with an equal enthusiasm. One wondered if any black spirits were standing behind our chairs, resentfully comparing their past with our present!

.   .   .   .

Since we had seen the hounds and the horses, it was no more than fitting that we should be shown a larger sample of their hunting country than our only day with these hounds had

116

vouchsafed, (our experiences having, as has been told, been limited to rushing to and fro, trying to 'mark to cry,' in the heart of a wood).

The Ford was at the door. It always is. Its superior relatives, the Rolls-Royce, the Panhard, the Lincoln, sit, like upper servants, in dignified seclusion, withdrawn from view, doing nothing. But, wherever a kindly fate had led us, we found that it was the Ford, like the pantry-boy, that did the work. Its task, this afternoon, was one that I should have hesitated to impose on the team of a mountain battery of Artillery. It was at first unexacting cross-country work, a stony cart-track through tillage fields, nothing serious for any hardy little car to complain of, until, without warning, it found itself engaged in a frontal attack on a grassy hill, at the sort of gradient that, if one were riding a horse, would involve a gradually lengthening vista of his spine, together with the immediate prospect of dismounting over his tail, accompanied by the saddle.

But the Ford flung itself at the hill, unfaltering, and when, feeling sympathetically breathless, we stood at gaze on the height, we real-

117

ised how very well worth while — for us, at all events — the effort had been. All round, as far as sight could travel, was green open country, beautiful to look at, and laid out, as if by a committee of M.F.H.'s, for Foxhunting. Dark patches on the wide outspread map told of woods, not so far apart as to rob a fox of a chance to catch his wind, not so near as to cut a hunt up into little bits. No rough hills, such as West Carbery knows, near enough to matter (though the Blue Ridge lay, a serrated wall of lapis-lazuli, on the horizon). No bogs anywhere. With such a country it is small wonder that Virginia has kept the faith, and follows the fox according to the straitest tradition of her Elizabethan forefathers!

. . . .

I am not without experience in hills. A bath-chair has run away with me down an incline that felt to be little short of the perpendicular. A young mare, full of enthusiasm and strange to the country, has taken me down the rocky side of a hill, well named the Hill of the Goat, 'in standing leps, the way the Devil came into Athlone.' And I have not forgotten following Mrs. Hitchcock's hounds in an Aiken buggy.

But these things pale before the descent of that grassy precipice.

'As the flight of a river that flows to the sea,' so, and with an ever-increasing swiftness, did the Ford glide downwards. It was not the face of the hill by which we had ascended. The idea was that some more hunters, out at grass in a field below, should be viewed, and it appeared to me that this side was rather the steeper. There were, I am sure, some fine horses in the field, but my attention was rivetted on the stream at the foot of the hill. I spoke of it, and my hostess said the car would get across it all right. It seemed improbable, but, apparently, in Virginia, as in Ireland, it is the improbable that happens.

What occurred, precisely, I cannot say. The ground sloped down to the stream in what felt like shelves, and the car dealt with it in a succession of frog-like springs. Three, I think, and a scramble.

. . . .

I knew a Literary Agent who said he had taken to Foxhunting in order to harden his nerve for encounters with Publishers, and he had proved its helpfulness. But I have not found a lifetime of foxhunting an adequate preparation for motoring in Virginia.

. . . .

Regretfully, early in April, we left the South, setting forth for the North on a morning of great beauty and great heat, so perfect a morning as might have deepened our regret at departure, had such deepening been possible. It was the unfortunate aspect of this American cruise that we left everywhere with regret. A sailor-servant wrote to his late master and lamented that he had 'been unable to have the painful pleasure of bidding G.B. to you, Sir.' That painful pleasure was only too frequently ours.

From our first days in New York, up to the time at which I have at this point arrived, it seemed as though we had no sooner found (in rapid succession) the most enchanting place in the world in which to pass the remainder of our lives, than an inexorable time-table dragged us up by the roots, reminding us of that 'Date' in New York which had been determined upon even before we left our native shore, forcing us to fill our trunks and cram our Go-pokes once more, and bid G.B. to those nice people who, where'er what the hymn calls 'our changeful lot' was cast, had taught us to deplore its changefulness.

Of American hospitality it might indeed be said that it had become a Fine Art, were it not that when one speaks of Fine Art one implies a grace that has involved something of effort, something also of elaboration and culture, while in the States we found the Open Door and the Welcome instinctive gestures. American hospitality, like American homes, is centrally heated, and its warmth comes from the heart.

CHAPTER XIV

I HAVE tried to express something of my awed admiration for that celebrated institution, the American Bathroom, and I now reflect that to another equally well-known triumph of American civilisation, the Telephone, I have not as yet paid my respects. I could do so more freely and with greater sincerity had not the moments at which I found myself reluctantly compelled to invoke its aid been filled with humiliation.

The remarkable speed of response to a call is in itself more than a little bewildering and upsetting. In Old World telephone-calls time is allowed, sometimes a considerable time, between the call and the operator's ring-back. It is possible to assemble the ideas, and to make sure that the required number is rightly remembered. And when the operating young lady, after a self-respecting interval, demands

the number, and, having corrected my pronun-
ciation and method of stating the figures, in-
forms me that I am 'through,' I can, in London,—(by speaking very slowly, and on a high
treble note, and through the nose, approximat-
ing my utterance to the official standard) —
generally ensure that I am understood.

In America everything seemed to conspire
against me. The instant response broke my
nerve, and when the call had been responded
to,— I speak more especially of efforts to com-
municate on business matters — it was shattering to find that little as my interlocutors
could understand me, I was unable to identify
so much as a word of the reply.

I remember with special mortification, if not
anguish, an attempt to arrange the despatch of
some of my luggage that had been temporarily
abandoned at one of my many ports of call.
I began to state my case, falteringly, because
I knew that every official term I used was in-
correct and most probably conveyed the wrong
meaning. A prolonged and plaintive mewing
responded, at whose purport I could not even
guess, but it was pitched on a high note, and
I diagnosed a female secretary. I asked if

I might be put on to the authority whom, in Ireland, I should call the Traffic Manager. There was a brief pause, and then followed a strange, almost sinister sound, a guttural snarl, uttered on the lowest bass note of which the human gullet is capable. The sounds were not only unintelligible but even alarming. If the lady official had sounded like a kitten, this response might have been made by an angry tiger with bronchitis. I believe I replied, incoherently, that I would fetch the house-maid — (and what the Tiger made of this singularly irrelevant rejoinder it is hard to imagine). That, at all events, was what I did. She, like myself, was Irish, but a more prolonged experience than mine had taught her not only the telephone timbre of voice, but also the needful vocabulary, and by her the affair was arranged.

I cannot but think (in spite of my personal failures) that the American telephone system is too perfect an instrument. It has combined with telegraphy to abolish the art of Letter-writing. Even letter-writing as far afield as to Europe has been undermined by its demoralising influence. A 'Week-end-letter-cable' is a poor substitute for a letter, and to telephone from Boston to, say, Paris or Vienna, for 'a little chat' as is the practice of a friend of mine, at the rate of about five dollars a minute, must, one would think, cramp the style.

. . . .

Our removal from Virginia to Madison, N.J., was accomplished with as little individual effort on our parts as though we had been grand pianos, or infants of a day old. We, with our baggage, combined the leading qualities of both. But the affair was put through with the marvellous efficiency, and the well-justified assumption of our helpless imbecility that we had by this time learnt to expect.

Thenceforward followed a period of varied activities which might fitly be characterised as strenuous or hectic, had not these adjectives been worn so threadbare by constant use that either would fail to meet the case. Daily (since a small show of pictures required my attendance) we took the long road from Madison to New York, a *trajet* that was turned from a toil into a pleasure by the perfect car that the kindness of our host had devoted to our service. We viewed that vast mausoleum of motor-cars, and super-rubbish-dump, the Manhattan Flats, and learned how, by the will of the great city, the unlovely swamp was changing its character. 'Let the dry land appear!' said New York, creatively, and it was so. And now immense buildings testify to its solidity. Probably, in the ages to come, the corpses of Fords will be usefully employed in constructing a way from the New World to the Old. Judging by what we have seen, they will pretty soon begin to shoulder each other over the edge of America, and only a little unanimity will be needed to accomplish the link.

Sometimes we flashed through the glittering Hudson tunnel, with cars flying before us and chasing after us, all at a single prescribed rate m.p.h. which admits of no hesitation. The pressure of a fever-temperature alone is comparable to that obsession of speed.

Then New York, and the temperature racing up again, in excited accord with the traffic. There fell a day when, as was not unusual, I was something late for a near-by engagement, and rather than face the agitations of two crossings, with the certainty that the baleful glare of the red light would meet me halfway

126

on each of them, I took a taxi, and very soon discovered that its driver was, even as I, an Exile of Erin. This, in New York was not surprising, but I cannot but think it was strange that out of the thousands of New York's taxi-men I should have chanced on one who, on enquiry, told me he came from a little country town, whence, long ago, I have had many a good hunt with the County Meath Hounds. There came another pause, and I spoke of a cousin who had lived there, and asked my driver if he had known him.

'Is it know him!' He appealed to high heaven. Then he turned and stared at me.

'Ye come of a fine family!' he declared, with a lighted face, and the green light came on, like a message from the green fields of Ireland.

(I am reminded of a recent and less amicable conversation with a 'jarvey,' a driver of an out-side-car in my own 'home-town' of Cork. Be-lieving me to be an ignorant stranger, he de-manded, as is customary in such a case, more than twice his rightful fare, and snatched a suit-case as a hostage. My train shrieked a summons; there was nothing for it but to yield the point and the disputed shilling. This I did, assuring the jarvey that I would take care never to employ him again. He replied suavely,

'My darlin' child, whenever I see ye I'll avoid ye!'

It was a poor consolation to tell him that I was not his darling child, but it was all I could do in the time, since the guard of my train, a personal friend, had come to fetch me.)

Sometimes on one of those dark spring evenings, the tunnel route was abandoned, in order that the visitors might be shown New York illuminated, become a city of fairy-land, blazing with jewelled light, all the beauty doubled and redoubled in the black water through which the huge steam-ferry-boat was rushing with nearly the speed of our motor, waiting now, one of a string of others, in the depths of the boat.

.   .   .   .

It was while we stayed at Madison that we were taken to see a dairy-yard and cow-byres of a spick-and-span perfection that made one think of a toy-shop super-toy, made for the instruction of a Brobdingnagian infant princess. Such prim and perfect squares of grass and gravel, with not a blade of grass or a pebble out of place, surrounding buildings that looked as if they had just been lifted out of careful German packing of tissue paper and clean pine shavings, with a picture on the lid of the box to show the proper arrangement of its contents. Nothing could be more supremely proper than the arrangements that we beheld. Nero's stables, in all their glory, were not, I am sure, lined with white porcelain slabs three or four feet square, nor could his horses — whatever they might do in chariot-racing — describe themselves as 'Class-leaders,' as was the proud title of some these Guernsey ladies.

We, who in our native wilds, also indulge in a dairy-farm, went away with the Inferiority Complex that had, since we landed in America, daily deepened and become normal, deeper and more normal than ever.

.   .   .   .

Somewhat we had heard of Tuxedo Park from various sources, but that the half had not been told to us we could scarce have believed had not its exclusive gates been hospitably opened to us, and we were admitted to spend a week-end within its borders.

129

We knew indeed that the Park was of the nature of a Reservation for millionaires, such a sanctuary as is the Yellowstone National Park, wherein, like bears and bisons, they could increase and multiply, existing beautifully, wrapped in segregated peace, safe from the storm and stress of the world without. What we were not prepared for was the beauty, not only of the Park, but also of the surrounding country. Hills and heather, lakes and fir-trees — it is easy to make lovely landscapes with these ingredients, and the farther we penetrated into the country beyond Tuxedo, the more romantic and reminiscent of the Highlands of Scotland it became.

Wonderful as was the wild country, it did not take us long to discover that all its beauties were concentrated — I had almost said intensified — within the limits of the Park. There, everything that good taste, and competent engineering, and (it need hardly be added) dollars, could do had worked hand in hand with Nature to create a sort of Earthly Paradise. It seemed to us, — humble ten-cent-enarians as we felt ourselves among the millionaires — that to live there must be some-

thing like living in heaven, without having recourse to any Other Place for Society! (Two
extremely enjoyable dinner parties having
convinced us of this fact.)

We spent two dazzled days there. We
glided round the lovely lake that is the centre
of the domain, on perfect roads, and went to
Sunday service in the perfect little church,
with its beautiful stained glass, and admirable
organ and choir; and saw sixty perfect Chow-
dogs, all the property of one triumphant
owner, all, I am convinced, first prize-winners,
whose coats and varied colours would turn any
enterprising furrier into an assassin. And we
were privileged to be shown a perfect labora-
tory, in which marvels are like silver in the
days of Solomon, and Nobel Prizes are, so to
speak, two a penny! I cannot refrain from at-
tempting to describe one of the wonders that
we were there shown. A ray of intense light
was directed at a white handkerchief; it shone
with a snowy radiance that would have been
the despair of an emulative laundress (if, indeed, ambition disturbs the seared soul of any
laundress). But when the handkerchief was
shaken and whirled in circles by the presiding

131

wizard, stripes of every colour of the rainbow illuminated it! One thought of the magical effect on a white-clad Corps de Ballet, at one moment still and white as a drift of snow, the next spinning, and whirling, and looking — or so one imagines would be the result — like so many prismatic zebras!

And we were shown the hospitality of a perfect Country Club, whose Committee rules and directs this wondrous and perfect settlement, and finally, were borne back to Madison, feeling that among all the perfections we had found nothing more perfect than the kindness of our entertainers.

CHAPTER XV

THE sedate and dignified repose of an University town was a remarkable change after the racing fever of New York, especially as a temporary accidental severance from all our possessions — that seemed, in the first delirium of despair, to be, most probably, eternal — set our last moments there aflame with anxiety.

The pain of farewell to New York, and to all the good friends and good fun that we had found there, was softened (and yet intensified) by a lunch party which had been thoughtfully planned by our kind Madison (and Virginian) host and hostess, so as not only to fill our last moments with enjoyment, but also to give us a completely new experience.

We were bound for the thirty-first story of

133

the Whitehall Building. It seemed that the
elevator would never stop. Floor after floor
twinkled by. I thought of a tale that I was
told in the Radnor Hunt country, of an Irish
groom who had been run away with on the
road by his master's best hunter. The master,
thinking with anxiety of his horse's legs, asked
if the pace had been considerable. The groom
replied, not without indignation, 'Is it go fast?
Sure the telegraph posts went by me like the
teeth of a comb!'

Thus it was, for us, with the floors of
the Whitehall Building. Having, however,
achieved the thirty-first without being obliged
to have recourse to oxygen, we dismissed the
fear of *vertige*, and addressed ourselves to the
view, moving from one to another window of
the spacious rooms of our host's Club, and
seeing new wonders from each of them. How
beautiful New York can look, only those can
understand who have seen her from the point
of view of the angels, and seen her, too, on such
a heavenly day of spring as was vouchsafed to
us. Far down the shining harbour Liberty
held aloft her torch. For the first time we
faced the Woolworth and Singer Buildings on

equal terms, and found them no less fine and impressive than when we gazed up at them from below. The great city, with its green spaces, and spaces of bright water, and up-soaring spires and towers, was displayed below us, sparkling in the blaze of sunlight, spreading as far as we could see, till it faded on the horizon in pale blue mist.

Across the open space in front of the Building we looked down on the tiny dots that meant men (and were reminded of the person who had gone so high in a balloon that all his uncles looked like ants) and marvelled that the motors, weaving their intricate courses to and fro, should move so slowly. If the grovelling uncles, crawling about down there, looked like ants, the cars were more like beetles, but beetles that went at so strangely leisurely a pace! Yet no one has ever accused New York automobiles of lack of speed! Then I thought of how airplanes, if only they are high enough, seem to drift across the sky, (while one knows that their rate of progress may be anything over ten thousand m.p.h.) and I bethought me of how slowly hounds seem to run, when viewed from a distance, (though how terribly fast, if one is riding after them with a bad start!) and my ignorant mind decided that there is, no doubt, a mathematical rule that can, for some people, explain these things.... Let me change the subject and repose my mind upon the comforting old formula,

'The higher the fewer'!

. . . .

I have diverged from the University Town with mention of which I began this chapter. New Haven was an experience for which I had to return in memory to a far-back visit to Oxford to find a fellow. Given into the keeping of two skilled and considerate authorities, who, as the hymn says, 'our weakness, pitying, saw,' and who did not expect from us too much intelligence, we were shown the University — Yale's earliest building, a reverently preserved relic of old Colonial times, came first, both chronologically and in interest, as was only fitting, and the lovely Wrexham Tower, in the Memorial Quadrangle, seen against the blue sky of spring, has stamped itself ineffaceably upon the memory.

Our time 'for to admire and for to see' was all too short, but, thanks to our acomplished guides, I think we can safely say that we skimmed the cream off all that was best worth seeing. Specially I remember the Art Galleries, with the wonderfully interesting American Revolution pictures, and miniatures of the chief men of that time, by Trumbull, which were for me a revelation, both in their high artistic merit, and in their illumination of the period. Also (such was my dark ignorance) to find, in a position of honour, a portrait of Berkeley, Bishop of Cloyne, (which is an old cathedral town in my own county of Cork) and to learn that he had come to New Haven, and had been a special patron of the then young University, gave a special thrill.

There was an atmosphere of old-world peace and dignity about the grave and stately buildings and quadrangles that — I must admit it — came as a surprise to one who had realised America's ardent present more vividly than her past. The tremendous 'Yale Bowl,' that can hold countless thousands, and yet is filled to the brim for one of the Homeric athletic contests between Yale and Harvard, and the vast Gymnasium, if more overwhelming in their vastness, were less unexpected, and were more in the order of what one had anticipated of Young America.

It was all very amazing to two reverential pilgrims, who were finally led back to a highbrow luncheon party of such massed learning as to intensify — though that was scarcely possible — that Inferiority Complex to which it is again impossible to avoid reference. But, that crushing complex notwithstanding, our moment to pose an unanswerable problem for the High Brows was approaching, and after lunch it arrived.

In order to give this memorable moment its due weight, I must retell an old story, whose authenticity as to its mere superficial facts is unassailable.

And this, I consider, deserves, and even demands a chapter to itself.

CHAPTER XVI

THERE is, in the south-west of the County Cork, a wild, almost uninhabited, and very beautiful tract of mountain country, that extends from Bantry Bay into Kerry, and onwards; Glengariff is its central point, and Castletown Bere Haven, (once, not long ago, an important station of the British Fleet) is another outpost of civilisation, planted in the wilderness near the mouth of Bantry Bay. Anyone who has read Froude's historical romance, 'The Two Chiefs of Dunboy,' will remember that one of them was O'Sullivan Bere, lord of all that country, and O'Sullivan's country is still the name it goes by. This story begins later than the time of the two Chiefs, in the year 1836, to be exact, nearly a hundred

139

years ago, when, it may safely be taken for granted, civilisation among these mountains was only such as had survived from the legendary times of Irish culture. One still can meet with beautiful manners among the 'mountainy' people. Courteous to the stranger, self-respecting, unhandicapped by any consciousness of such superficials as bare feet or rags. In 1836 Castletown Bere was a very small and primitive village, untouched even by such civilisation as Bantry knew. A very old gentleman who, as Coroner, had occasionally to make his way into the mountains, has told me that he had seen a cabin built around a single big block of stone, which served as a table, and was the only furniture that the place possessed. (But primitive as it is, that wild country has a long history, and it is well known that it was out somewhere on that desolate coast that the Prophet Jeremiah landed when he brought Pharaoh's daughter with him to Ireland. And this must be true, because every second boy in the County of Cork answers to the name of Jerry!)

In, or near, the village of Castletown, at this time, 1836, there lived a doctor named Arm-

THE 'MOUNTAINY MAN'

strong. To him, one morning, early, came a man of the hills, a 'mountainy man,' to say his wife was ill, and to ask for help. The man told the Doctor that he had made all the haste he could, and had come over the mountains by as near a way as he could make. And then, I can imagine, with shyness and some hesitation, he showed the Doctor a little shoe — a tiny little bit of a shoe, not quite three inches long. He said it was in the dawning that he had seen it on the grass, on a high pass in those lonesome hills. He didn't much care for the little shoe. But it might bring luck, and he hadn't liked to leave it, lying on the short mountain grass; but again, it mightn't. I can imagine him turning it about uncomfortably, before he ventured to hint that it must have been dropped by one of the Good People — a Cluricaun may be, a lad that if you could catch a hold of him, you might make him show you where he had his crock of gold hidden. Cluricauns (or Leprehauns) are the fairies' cobblers, 'and I wouldn't doubt,' says the mountainy man, 'but this lad was mending the shoe for one o' them, and he heard meself coming, and he legged it away then and left the brogue-een after him!'

Some such explanation, I expect, the man offered the Doctor, and then, with all the satisfaction one feels in making a handsome present of something that one wants to get rid of, he presented the Doctor with the little shoe.

This is the true history of the entrance of the Fairy Shoe into mortal society. The Doctor gave it to his sister, who married Judge Fitz-henry Townshend, who was my Grandfather's first cousin, and she left it, with its history carefully set down and attested, to her daughter, and it came at last to her great-grand-daughter, and she—like the mountainy man—didn't altogether fancy it, so she gave it to my sister (and I think it has brought luck instead of taking it away).

. . . .

The little shoe came with us across the Atlantic. It seemed to us that in America, if anywhere, we should meet people with open minds, not afraid to be interested in what they could not explain.

And we found that we had not been mistaken. The Fairy Shoe had, everywhere, a reception that was at once enthusiastic and respectful. But it was at our High Brow parties at Yale that it received the discerning and un-prejudiced examination to which it is justly entitled. Let me try to describe it.

It is made of black — or what once may have been black — leather as fine and nearly as thin as silk; and yet it is real leather, that looks like the strong leather of which our countrymen's brogues are made, were it seen through a diminishing glass. It is shaped like a brogue, but is unnaturally narrow for its length. The sole at its widest is no more than three-quarters of an inch wide, while it is two-and-three-quarters inches long. (How slim and slender must be the fairy feet!)

There are little holes in the 'uppers' for laces. The workmanship is incredibly fine. There are signs of wear at the heel, which is wrinkled a little, and the sole is dinted, no doubt with the rocks of the mountains, where its wearer 'fleeted the time away as in the Golden Age'! (For those who do not know what a 'brogue' is like, this drawing is as accurate as I could make it.

The impressive fact about the exhibition at Yale of this 'enigma from the world antique'

143

was the cool and courageous acceptance of it as a problem for which a solution might or might not be found. It occurred to no one to dismiss with derision what could not be explained. No one made the suggestion that it was a doll's shoe — or a baby's. (A doll's shoe, found on a desolate mountain pass, forty miles from any town! A baby's shoe made of leather, and not an inch wide!) These conjectures have many times been the refuges of the destitute in intelligence, but Yale offered no such futile insults to the Cluricaun's brogue! Five, it may have been six, men of learning, occupants of those Seats of the Mighty, the Chairs of the University, placed themselves round a table in the centre of which sat the little shoe in solitary state, complacently challenging investigation, and not even that Professor whose especial subject was the fancies and follies of Folklore, could suggest a solution that conformed with the facts. Wisdom has sometimes the courage to admit itself baffled.

I have talked to an illiterate Kerry peasant who owned a small farm deep in the mountains above Killarney. His farm is beside a little lake, with (so I had been told) a fairy island on

144

THE FAIRY SHOE

it, and—(so I had been further told)—'anny-one that'd land on it 'd get a sthroke.' I asked the farmer if he had ever seen the fairies. He said no, he hadn't seen them himself. 'But,' he said, 'my father seen them, and they that high' (he indicated about two feet from the ground) 'and with red caps on them. And,' he added, 'they having green faces.'

Now it is a singular fact that a short time before this, I had read an article in 'Light,' in which it was said that Sir Arthur Conan Doyle had formed the opinion that there were two tribes of fairies, and one tribe had blue faces, and the other green.

A lady who lives at Glengariff, has told me of the reluctance of one of her workmen to cut timber in a certain wood, because he said the fairies came about him there, and frightened him. And she has shown me a picture, painted while he was her guest, by that Irish poet, and painter, and see-er, who is best known by the mystic initials A E, in which a fairy boat, with fairy beings in it, is drifting on the waters of that most lovely harbour; and his friend and hostess said he had painted it from life.

I have had the pleasure of meeting A E; he

told me how, on the Dublin mountains, he had made many sketches of the beings he had seen there; he said that he had shown these to an old woman in the County Mayo (who also had 'the Sight') and she had picked out some of his drawings, rejecting others, as being pictures like the fairies she had seen.

Moreover — this for the incredulous of the New World — a visitor to Ireland from the States, has given me a full account of how she and three friends were all put astray on a mountain in Mayo by 'Horns of Elfland, faintly blowing'; and in the air round them laughter and crying, where was no one to laugh or cry; and twice by little figures, far away, beckoning to them, for whom my friend and her companions searched, believing they might be lost children, and found not.

. . . .

One more incident in the career of the Fairy Shoe I must give, and I will then undertake not to recur to the subject.

The experiment of seeing what a psychometrist could make of it was suggested, and wrapped in a disguising swaddling of paper, it was given to one of those on whom the mysterious gift has been bestowed of receiving from some inanimate object intimations of its past. In this case the resulting emotions were vague and troubled. The Sensitive spoke disquietedly of a Strange People, of warriors, of fighting, and of horses often, of galloping horses — bewilderment — nothing definite.

Had the two Chiefs of Dunboy ridden out against each other over that high mountain pass? Or were the galloping horses fairy horses, made of bulrushes — as is the fairy way — and ridden to battle by warring tribes of a strange people, some with blue faces, and some with green faces?

CHAPTER XVII

IT WAS at New Haven that my sister and I had to part company and to pursue our buccaneering courses henceforth singly (my grief at the parting being much intensified by the fact that she returned to New York with my railway ticket to Providence in her pocket, and was gone beyond recall before I discovered the loss). Moodily, I took another ticket, and bade farewell to Yale with all the inevitable regret that is the consequence of making new and delightful friends in the pauses of a pilgrimage only to part from them in a few brief hours.

I like the friendly American habit of offering to a new acquaintance the assurance that the meeting is a pleasure; but I should like it more if I knew the suitable rejoinder. (As an Irish Protestant farmer excused himself when rebuked by his clergyman for not answering the responses in Church. 'I'm very sorry, your Reverence, but I don't rightly know the repartee.') Thus it was with me. When, as was usually the case, I was unable to get first off the mark with the courtesy, all repartee failed me save a murmured and futile Thank you, which is very inadequate and does not even suggest reciprocity. A young friend in the Foreign Office told me that when someone said to him, 'I am very pleased to meet you,' he was accustomed to reply by saying brightly, 'People generally are!' But I think such a response demands the nerve acquired in international 'conversations.'

. . . .

I have already commented on the attractiveness of much American architecture, and in Providence I saw many very fine old Colonial Mansions, that, in their sober, balanced dignity, are typical of its calm and serious past, and of the old-time and God-fearing men who called their town by its old-time and God-fearing name. Now these seem to hold themselves aloof from the immense, striving modern city that has changed for them so entirely the aspect of the world they once knew.

In Providence (or near it) it was that I had my first run in a racing-car. I was asked if I liked speed. Trusting that the Power that had sponsored the city would befriend me, I replied in the affirmative, and found myself, practically simultaneously, on the horizon. Providence, however, proved kind, and as soon as consciousness returned I was able to appreciate the Jacobs' Hill Foxhound Kennels, which were, I found, established on or about the horizon in question, and to admire their planning as well as their inmates.

(Also, with the return of the power of thought, to resolve that the next time such an enquiry was made to me to be more guarded. And, in this connection, I may quote the comment of an old friend of mine, in respectful censure of her Creator, when a motor-car first swam into her ken.

'Glory be to the most High God! That He should make such a thing, and place it on the earth!')

.   .   .   .

I think it was on the afternoon of this day that, returning from a wedding, I enjoyed the entirely unexpected diversion of a hunt.

(Quite, I hasten to say, without any connection with the hounds I had seen in the morning.)

It was a very smart wedding, in a very large and fine church which was quite filled with guests. At the porch we were received by a bevy of beautiful young men, all wearing in their buttonholes the white flowers of blameless lives, and these, while awaiting the arrival of their official charges, the Bridesmaids, armed the female guests to their seats, gallantly irrespective of age, or beauty to correspond with their own. A polite and graceful custom that now, or so I am given to understand, again obtains in the British Isles although at one time it had fallen into desuetude, the place of the beautiful young Ushers having been taken by vergers, or by elderly male relatives, who, worried, overheated, and anxiously shielding from harm their silk hats, hustled the Bride's people into the Bridegroom's side of the church, and vice versa.

The wedding was over, we had reached home, and were hurrying through the garden to release the four little dogs, necessarily immured during their mistress's absence and volubly resenting it, when, almost incredulous that we saw aright, we beheld a small drab rabbit seated on the gravel walk in the state of entire immobility into which the unmolested rabbit is wont to fall. One would as soon, in this *milieu*, have expected to meet a giraffe, and, for a moment, it seemed possible that, like the Guernsey dairy, it was one of the super-toys of a millionaire-child, despised and abandoned. So deep was its trance of repose that we advanced upon it unobserved, and had nearly seized it by the ears — which is the correct procedure — when it woke to violent activity, and for some time, oblivious of our wedding garments, we pursued it from bush to bush round the garden. We had surrounded it in a corner — there were three of us — and were on the verge of success, when it broke our line, and darting through the entrance gates, it crossed the road and fled into a neighbouring garden.

In an instant, as, one is told, vultures scent or spy from afar the dead camel, fourteen little boys (more or less) were materialised, and the chase, augmented by them and by a widowed charwoman with sporting tastes, stormed on.

Four crowded minutes, 'on the grass' (of the neighbouring garden) 'without a check, boys!' ensued before the rabbit again broke the enemy line, and bolted across the road once more. By this time the little dogs had realised something of what was toward. From the farther side of the garden gate their cries of anguish rent the air. At intervals, over the top of the gate, two white snouts told of hopeless effort on the part of the Sealyhams. Two black ones, poked under it, bespoke the despair of the Dachshunds. How cruel it was to keep them out of the fun! And yet the differing point of view of the rabbit could not be forgotten. In the end the quarry was coerced into the garage, where it was left to be collected by the chauffeur, and it is now, probably, what I have heard spoken of as the 'gated infant' of his children (unless, indeed, he preferred to augment with it the family larder).

The episode was a great mental refreshment, and gave us something interesting to talk about during the performance of two excessively dull and badly acted plays to which we went that evening. I do not remember their names, but I understood that they were the work of two of America's leading dramatists. In one of these a maniac seaman is confronted by a procession of the ghosts of his murdered victims (stout fellows, not a man of them walking less than two hundred pounds), which so upsets him that in a fit of rather inconsequent remorse he murders his sister, or his father, possibly both, but of this I am not certain. Of the second play I can remember nothing, save that at the first moment that was decently possible, we 'passed upon the midnight without pain.'

.   .   .   .

I had heard much of the beauties of Newport, R.I.; of its rockbound shore on which the waves of the Atlantic break in direct rebound from the no less rocky shores of my own country, and of the palatial mansions that glorify its heights. Unfortunately, it happened that, on the appointed day, Ireland had sent, with the waves, a sample of her worst weather, rain, wind, and fog, a combination that I had thought peculiar to our coast. As we sped along the admirable roads I could but just see through the rain the white line of breakers on the rocks below us, and the invisible, (though

154

no doubt palatial) mansions, each wore a shroud of impenetrable mist.

The special one for which we were bound for long eluded us completely. It was only after prolonged groping through dark plantations, and struggling up rain-enveloped hills, that we ran it to ground. There, indeed, we found the warmth of welcome that the weather had omitted to offer, and I forgot to regret that so far as the beauty of Newport landscape was concerned the expedition had proved literally, 'a wash-out.'

It occurs to me here, by a connection of ideas less far-fetched than may seem to be the case, to pause, in order to enquire where and how American women have learned the secret of eternal youth? That many of them possess it is beyond contradiction.

How often have I not been stupefied by the discovery that the sylph-like being with the rose-leaf complexion, to whom I had been speaking as to a recent *débutante*, is the mother of six, of whom the eldest is just engaged to be married? It fell to me once to have been invited to lunch by letter, and to have the invitation renewed in person by one whom —

very justifiably, as I still think — I took to be a child of sixteen, the daughter of the lunch-giver. I said kindly

'Please tell your mother that I shall be delighted —

I was interrupted.

'But it is *I* who —'

In fact I was talking to the principal in the affair, who subsequently showed me her children because I had demanded '*pièces de conviction.*'

. . . .

Four little dogs have been incidentally spoken of, and it is but right and fitting that persons of their importance should have fuller mention. To one who has the habit of little dogs — and I had left two sorrowing small white ladies at home — it is almost painful to be in the house with their like and not to find oneself the first object of consideration. It brings to mind too acutely those forsaken ones, whose devotion has been bereft of its object. The dogs of the house eye the visitor politely, and possibly offer venal attentions at meals, but their spiritual remoteness is unmistakable. In vain in this house, in which the dogs held so paramount a place, I tried humbly to make myself agreeable to them, and in especial to a tiny dachshund, like a black satin worm, with a nose like a stiletto, and a tail tapering to a practically invisible point. My overtures were ignored. A lady Sealyham did indeed occasionally condescend to avail herself of my knee, but, I fear, only in order to command a more comprehensive view of the tea-table. The remaining trio ignored my existence.

But I thought of my little Taspy, at home, and of the welcome that she was keeping for me, and

> '*I sigh'd and said amang them a':* —
> '*Ye are na Mary Morison!*'

(as Robbie Burns has sung; though, as we say in Ireland, I wonder was he trusting to the one young lady!)

I cannot refrain, presently, from introducing into these rambling reminiscences, one short chapter that is a memorial of one short life. I know that Taspy has friends on the farther side of the water who will read about her with interest as well as sympathy. And those who love their own dogs will, I believe, forgive what

157

may seem the irrelevance of her story. For those who are (perhaps fortunately for them) immune of this weakness, it will be easy to close the book.

CHAPTER XVIII

SHE slid into the family almost imperceptibly. I had lost in sad succession three well-loved little dogs, a mother, a daughter, an aunt, and I had said that no more should my heart be torn, and for the future I would live alone, dog-less.

But a friend of many years, who has been for long my prime-minister in kennels and stables (and, perchance, knows me better than I know myself) thought otherwise, and took steps accordingly.

.   .   .   .

I said

'How did you know that it was exactly the sort of little dog I like?'

The answer came, gravely and respectfully.

'I knew you'd fancy her, Miss, because the Mother is a little small low bitch.'

The reason was good. I recognised the acuteness of the psychology that had probed my inclinations and divined so accurately my taste. '*Matre pulchra, filia pulchrior.*'

The daughter, when my eyes first beheld her, sat on the floor, looking like a small circular shape of blancmange, topped with marmalade. But her eyes. Even at two months old, those burning brown eyes were already aflame with intelligence; the brow above them was broad, and as round as an apple.

I said I would give her the old family name of Cozy, and she should be entered in the succession as Cozy the Fourth. It was, I knew, tactless to enquire further as to her breeding, but I could at least ask her godfather whence she had come.

'Ryan the saddler,' I was told, and that he would be honoured if I would accept the pup as a present.

I consented to do so. Later, a suitable interval having elapsed, I made the appropriate gesture of response. Lacking, indeed, in imagination or originality, yet received — so I understood from the godfather — with the appreciation that ten shillings can sometimes inspire.

All was now in order, and Cozy the Fourth was installed as prospective House-dog in chief.

. . . .

The position was never subsequently questioned, even though there arrived, some ten days later, another little creature of similar age and type — (it should be mentioned that both were of the small variety of smooth fox-terrier) — but of high Stud-book lineage. It even was 'in the book' as 'Princess Mary of ——' (it matters not where). It arrived in a satin-lined basket, with a blue ribbon round a little neck that a wedding-ring could almost have spanned. The little head, neatly divided, half black, half white, ended in a nose as sharp as a pen; the little body would fit, curled up, into the palm of a hand. It was obviously impossible to call such a thing Princess Mary, and as 'Prinkie' the new arrival was received into the family.

Of Prinkie — (secondary in these memories, as in all other things, to her comrade) — it may be briefly stated that the airs and affectations inspired by the satin-lined basket have coloured her character through life. She is the dog who imposes upon visitors, leaping, uninvited, light as a fly, upon laps, and there falling into atti-

161

tudes that suggest a trance of passion, and impel the gratified stranger to remark,

'This little dog seems to have taken quite a fancy to me! *May* I give her a piece of cake?'

. . . .

The alteration in the style and title of one puppy had soon to be repeated in the case of the other. Cozy was a name that for several generations had been worn with distinction by respectable and law-abiding little dogs. It was regrettable to find that it was now being dragged into disrepute by the latest of the series. A curt entry in my diary states *'Puppies supremely filthy and shoe-stealing. Have changed Cozy's name to Taspy because of her extreme naughtiness.'*

'Taspy' is Irish for impudence and exuberance, with a dash of naughtiness thrown in, and these qualities culminated on an occasion when Prinkie's dinner had seemed desirable to the late Cozy the Fourth in addition to her own. I whipped her, (being of the school of King Solomon in the matter of the rod). There was no uncertainty in her mind as to her crime. I had arrived just in time to view the last convulsive gobblings of the stolen meal.

But even at the age of some three or four months she had made up her mind as to her rights and my privileges. Whipping was not to be one of the latter. At this time she was no bigger than a kitten, but she took up a defensive position in a corner, and with absurd infant growls, exhibited two perfect rows of tiny teeth like seed pearls.

Discipline had to be maintained, and the appropriate chastisement followed, but

'the foeman's steel could not bring that proud soul under.'

To the end of her too-short life, she never, without indignant protest, submitted her little person to correction.

Yet it must be said that no little dog ever had a more sensitive conscience, or a more perfect grasp of that fatal knowledge of Good and Evil that has proved so disastrous to the children of Eve. To see Taspy crawl, *ventre à terre*, across the kitchen, after a raid on the forbidden fruit of the scullery bucket, was to see, as in a Miracle Play, Contrition and Guilt made tangible. With stricken face and melting eyes she has crouched at my feet, acknowledging that her sin was ever before her. But did I

163

then (remembering the advice of the Wise King) exhibit the rod, in an instant the penitent has become a fury, and because to bite me (as I deserved) was, even in passion, impossible for her, she has flung herself on the nearest live thing, dog or hen, and — as I have heard it expressed — has 'eased her temper' upon it.

In all other respects her character could be charged with but one flaw, and that, as I think, a venial one. The pleasures of the table were for her irresistible, but my own conscience cannot be absolved of confederacy. I know that, at family meals, to pass titbits, however secretly, to dogs, is not done by the best people. But for my part, I find that my self-respect will not let me play so selfish a part as to gormandise uninterruptedly, regardless of the silent watcher beside my chair.

. . . .

All bones she regarded as her right and perquisite, but it chanced one day that a valuable specimen had escaped her notice and had been acquired by Prinkie. This outrage was suffered until my repressive presence was removed. Then to me, in the adjoining room, came sounds of battle, and a swing-door banged. I found Prinkie on her feet, staring at the door, bereft of the bone.

I said in a terrible voice,

'Where is Taspy?'

The swing-door was pushed open a very little way, a small head appeared, with ears laid back, and coldly submissive eyes. In the mouth was an enormous bone. Nothing was said on either side. The mouth opened, the bone was dropped. The head withdrew as quietly as it had appeared; the door banged once more.

Restitution having been made, the affair ended, but I have reason to believe that the bone's stormy career closed in Taspy's collection.

But often bullying, and always greedy though it can't be denied she was, that little dog had the peculiar quality of charm and personality that speedily established her in the honourable position of Head-dog. The others made no protest. The first mouthful of a shared repast was always hers; her prior claim to my lap was never disputed. Taspy was Head-dog.

. . . .

Beyond the minor social amenities, common to most dogs — saying Please, and Sitting-up — she had one accomplishment, invented and instituted by herself. In moments of boredom, greed, or desire to attract attention, she would suddenly spin round and round, like a top, on her own axis, at a pace that resolved her into a mere blur of whiteness, and then, reversing, would continue thus to whirl for, perhaps, a couple of minutes. This performance she refused to vulgarise by exhibition to order. No bribe could induce her to do more than follow her tail in a languid circle for the edification of lookers-on.

Inferior to her love for me, though intense and enduring, she cherished two subsidiary passions. The object of one of these was a huge grey Persian cat, whom, at first sight, she immediately adored. But the adoration was unrequited. In vain she smiled, and wagged, and wooed the monster with every wile in her *répertoire;* he continued to regard her with the unspeakably bitter and heartless eyes peculiar to his race, and would certainly have assaulted her had he been free to do so. Why she loved him will ever be a mystery. To no other cat

166

did she pay the faintest attention. For her own sake she was permitted to meet him no more, but once, through a window, she viewed him, stalking in stern meditation in his owner's garden, and she thrilled and stiffened until had one touched her little tail I believe it would have hummed and sung like the string of a 'cello.

The other passion was for an elderly lady of her own breed, named Folly. This also, was unreciprocated, but was endured. Taspy's singular method of declaring her love was to spring to and fro past Folly's nose, bestowing on it at each spring a passing lick, while the loved one stood still, with half-open jaws, growling without intermission, the last act in the scene being the prostration of the adorer, who, casting herself on her side at Folly's feet, would lie, 'Down-deepening from swoon to swoon,' fainting 'like a dazzled morning moon.'

. . . .

I have said nothing of her looks. They were strictly unorthodox, and disobeyed all Show-Bench rules; none the less, as a good judge said of her, 'A prettier little dog never wagged a tail!' While another declared that Taspy's eyes were the most beautiful he had ever seen in the head of any living creature. More than this can scarcely be said.

To kill mice and rats, and to chase rabbits and lawn tennis balls, are functions proper to all well-educated little dogs; Taspy's activity in such pursuits was abnormal, and her speed inferior only to that of wireless waves (which travel, as I have learnt, at the rate of 168,000 miles a second). When she competed no other creature could secure the ball; if, by human trickery, it had been given to a competitor, nothing short of the onslaught of a torpedo could equal the furious speed with which she would charge, and snatch the ball from the jaws of the rival.

. . . .

I believe there may still be some who deny to dogs the possession of a soul, of something that outlives the death of the body and retains the personality that informed it in this world. If to have psychic sight, and the power 'to discern spirits,' of which St. Paul speaks, implies, as I believe, a kindred soul, to this little dog of mine that power was given. Indeed, she was not the first of my dogs to be thus endowed. I have written elsewhere of two small white ladies, Candy and Sheila, and of these Sheila possessed 'The Sight.' More than once after Candy's death I have seen Sheila, sitting in her basket, fix her eyes on something low down, at the door. Round the room something has come towards her. I could see her eyes follow it. Then, with very low growls, she has stolen from the basket, and crept under a sofa, just as she had been wont to do when Candy, incarnate, had played the same trick on her.

And Taspy, greedy, material little being though she was, had the same strange gift, denied to Prinkie, denied also, alas, to me. Many times I have seen her wonderful eyes, glowing, fix themselves on someone by me unseen. She has turned as the visitor moved, gazing, with small bewildered growls, into what was to me empty space. Twice she has reached out her head, sniffing, trying to catch the wind of what was so apparent to her, and once, when the visitor stood behind me, Taspy has risen in my lap, growling still, staring over my shoulder. And once the visitor brought Candy with her, and Taspy glared and raged,

169

and barked, and forgot to be frightened, indignant at the intrusion of the stranger spirit.
But afterwards I have known whom she saw.

.   .   .   .

A more single-hearted little creature never
lived. Given at once, supreme and unfaltering
to the end of her little life, was her devotion to
me. Such a love, utterly pure and whole-
souled, is a gift of which it is difficult to feel
worthy. One asks oneself how it can be repaid;
one feels that it were better that a millstone
were hanged about one's neck than that one
should 'offend one of these little ones.'
And yet the time must sometimes come
when a journey has to be made, and the wor-
shipper must be left behind. Or, worse, when
illness is upon them, and what must seem like
senseless tortures of food and medicine have to
be insisted upon, and the touching, unresentful
endurance of the victim cuts one to the heart.
Perhaps they comprehend more and better
than one thinks. One can only *faintly trust
the larger hope.*

.   .   .   .

These inadequate jottings must cease, yet
those who love dogs will understand how

memories crowd, memories that provoke the perilous laughter that can be so near tears. I think of Taspy's madness for motoring, and of that day when — as little more than a puppy — she had been successfully eluded and left behind. Half a mile from home, at half-speed on a steep hill, the driver looked down over the wheel, and said,

'Taspy is following us, Miss!' and in triumph she joined the party.

And, supremely, I think of that May morning, not a year ago, when as the White Star tender-steamer slid up to the pier at Queenstown, I saw her in my brother's arms, her eyes, like those of the little dog in the fairy tale, as big as mill wheels, scanning the face of each traveller arriving from the United States, until the one she well knew she had come to meet was seen, and the whole little creature became ecstasy made absolute.

. . . .

Of her last illness, there is little to say, only that for nearly a month we fought for her life with all the weapons that love and care and skill could bring to the struggle.

In the end all that we could do for her was

171

to give her a safe conduct over the Border to
join that company that had sometimes come
so near to her. I sat with a finger on the little
ebbing pulse, and could only thank God when
it ceased.

.   .   .   .

There may be some who sympathise, and
are in like case with me, who have not read
some lines that my cousin, Kathleen Conyng-
ham Greene, has written, which go to the heart
of the matter. They are called 'Fulfilment'; I
should like to quote them all, but the last verse
must suffice.

'And there the little ghosts that trot behind us,
      Untiring, from the past,
May at some golden, glittering corner find us,
      And know it Heaven at last.' [1]

[1] China Cats, and Other Beasts in Rhyme. Philip Allan &
Co., Ltd.

CHAPTER XIX

ONE day we motored to Boston. This was my
first visit to that historic 'Home of the Bean
and the Cod,' since, during the pause, on our
outward journey, that our ship made there, we
did not go ashore, and the sole record of our
brief sojourn was a photograph of my sister
and myself, taken on behalf of a Boston news-
paper, of so singularly unattractive, even re-
pulsive a character, that had it come to the
eyes of authority, we should probably have
been refused permission to land.

It was in the course of this drive — though
I am unable to specify the locality — that
I realised the scale on which industries such
as with us would come under the head of

173

Petite Culture, are run in the States. I noticed from afar two large spaces of pure white, which, at first, I could only take to indicate a strictly local fall of snow, reserved — as in the case of Gideon's Fleece — to two especial spots. The alternative idea then occurred that these were the drying grounds of some eminent laundress, who whitened without disintegrating. It was only when we drew abreast that I found that what I saw were thousands of snow-white ducks, seated on a large sheet of water, which they covered from shore to shore, as a table is covered by a table-cloth. They sat there motionless. It seemed to me that they were wedged together so tightly they could not move. It was hard to realise that they were alive. Had I been told that they were celluloid toys, and were destined to reconcile the reluctant baby to the rigours of the bath, I should have found it easier to believe.

. . . .

We drove into Boston by the Fenway, which seemed to me the most beautiful and unexpected approach imaginable to a great city, and with that superb overture, the quiet, old-world, almost Early English, little provincial town that Hawthorne and Emerson and Washington Irving had built in my mind, crashed in ruins....

I am afraid it may be said of me that I indulge in reckless superlatives, yet I cannot prevent myself from saying that the great house on that street of great houses, Beacon Street, to whose owner's delightful hospitality I was indebted for my visit to Boston, is the finest example of a fine period — approximately, Queen Anne to George II — that I have ever seen. Few, if any, English or Irish town-houses of its time can exceed this Boston mansion in dignity, in proportion, in what I can only call ordered splendour. And among its splendours I cannot forbear to signalise the great library, with its rich lining of books, that are presided over by a Hoppner portrait at one end, and a Raeburn at the other, illuminated, in pleasing anachronism, by the soft radiance of electric light, just as in the rest of the house the eighteenth and the twentieth centuries have come to each other's aid — '*les extrêmes se touchent!*'

. . . .

Fenway Court, the remarkable monument
175

that Mrs. Jack Gardner raised to Art, and to herself, must be respectfully mentioned, but is far too tremendous a place for casual comment by the ignorant and unlearned. I may at least speak of the marvellous *coup d'œil* of flowers and fountain, columns and arches, that, on the opening of the great entrance door, gave this visitor her first shock of admiration, and she is grateful for this opportunity of saying how immeasurably the interest and pleasure of her visit was increased by the cultured expounding of the wonders of this wonderful place by one supremely qualified for the task — its Custodian.

Unforgettable is the memory of the great Sargent picture of the Spanish Dancer. One sees it at the end of a darkened corridor with a low arched roof — (that, at least, is how it has stayed in my mind). It feels like looking direct into Spain. In Burgos I have seen such an interior — and indeed, in Ireland, too, though there the dancer was lacking to the scene. Gradually through the gloom and the tobacco smoke the faces of the watching men in the background begin to appear. They sit there silent, rather stupefied; one can see that

176

they are thinking of nothing, just seeing from the eyes outwards, visualising the curving figure of the dancing girl. In Spain they will probably come out of their silence to discuss her; in Ireland, even if such a figure were possible there, I think they would be more likely to talk of the price of pigs.

.   .   .   .

For any Irish man or woman to propose a visit to the United States is to find him or herself loaded by 'the neighbours' with messages to innumerable relatives, quite regardless of such geographical inconveniences as the fact that New York is not very near San Francisco, nor is Boston a suburb of Chicago. For our Munster people America is infinitely less remote than England.

'Ah, I wouldn't wish me little gerr'l 'd go so far from me —' (this when 'a place' in London has been suggested) 'and sure she'll be going to Boyshton-Mass with another little gerr'l in the spring.'

I had been successful in seeing several 'little gerr'ls,' but I had no mission for 'Boyshton-Mass.' Nevertheless on the morning after my arrival there, there came for me a telegram of the length of the average British letter, such a telegram as I have only received in the United States. Its purport was to tell me that one Bridget Collins — (that was not the name, but 'twill serve) — who had, long years ago, been in my mother's service, was in a situation not far away, and 'there would be' (said the telegram, soaring into poetry) 'a song in her heart if she could see you!'

A trysting place was suggested, and although the name given awoke no responsive chord, I promised to meet the suppliant there. At the tryst was Bridget Collins, with a posy of flowers in her hand, and a little book of poems from her lady, who was, she told me, 'the only one she ever seen whom she'd even with the Mistress!' ('The Mistress' was my mother.) And she had a greeting for me that made Time retrace his steps, and brought back the sunny old days, when, as Rossetti says, we all were 'Young and Together.'

'But,' said I, 'your name wasn't Bridget?'

'It was Julia, Miss, the Mistress called me, for she having two other girls in the house by the name of Bridget, but sure it was Bridget was my name through all!'

A 'LITTLE GERR'L' IN THE ROUGH

She hadn't lost her soft County Cork voice, nor the pretty manners that haven't all died out yet (in spite of Socialism and the importance of the Irish Free State!). Then it came back to me. Yes, of course! I thought, Julia! who had been a parlourmaid, and whom Patsey, my then fox-terrier, used to be incited by me to bite, when he sat on my lap during dessert, and poor Julia was nervously putting down the finger-glasses; and I remember also how she had said of him, little snob that he was, 'For all he's so cross to me in the parlour, he's very favourable to me in the kitchen!' So Julia and I talked together of old times, and she asked after Master Jack, (and wasn't he the lovely child, and didn't the Mistress dote down on him!). And Miss Hildegarde, and was she married yet? And Master Aylmer, that was arch always — (which being interpreted means that he had a gift for mischief and getting into scrapes that endeared him to all the countryside). I told her of them all, and remembered how an old woman had said of my poor Mother's disreputable family, part in reprobation, part in praise (but mostly, I venture to think, in praise) 'Thim 'd gallop the woods all the night, like the deer! And the marri'd gentlemen the worst of all!'

The married gentleman was 'Master Aylmer,' married at two and twenty, who has gone, and will 'gallop the woods' no more.

CHAPTER XX

THERE were not many sights or doings, among these American experiences of ours, that were more to my fancy than the visits to the several Packs of Foxhounds that I was permitted to make. It was happiness to put on a white kennel-coat again, and stand in the kennel-yards among the beloved hounds, and hear the biography of each, and listen to the serious encomiums bestowed on them, individually, in due order of merit, by their huntsmen, while the hounds listened with equal gravity, though their beautiful eyes did not leave my face, because I had a pocketful of broken biscuit.

The Myopia was a pack that (in my narrow-minded way) I could admire without reservations. The hounds were all practically pure

English Foxhound in type, well-bred ladies and gentlemen all of them, with necks and shoulders, bone and feet, fit for Peterborough, and the manners of the best society; in short, as I once heard said in another connection, 'the manners that belongs to them!' (only it was said in grim disapproval of a very rude and offensive human, to whose standard of language and deportment no foxhound could sink).

The kennels also. I think I may safely say that among all the well-planned and well-appointed kennels that I visited, two were pre-eminent, and the Myopia Establishment was one of them.

After the hounds (very properly!) the horses. But not, in this case, the Hunt horses, the Stud Farm of a former M.F.H., where, for me, the Tenth Commandment, already much damaged, was finally shattered to atoms.

If it is desired to see absolute perfection in form, balance, and grace, (as well as fitness for the special task of life) such precious gifts are not easily met with, but I believe a young thorough-bred horse comes nearer the case than any other four-legged creature under the sun (if not two-legged!). It is only necessary to

think of the animals that have been so cou-
rageously captured by photography in the wild
places where they were born and bred, to
realise how immensely Art has improved upon
Nature. The rhinoceros, the wart-hog, the
baboon, the absurdly disproportioned giraffe;
even the lion, whose most recent portraits —
after a satisfactory meal of zebra — suggest, as
to figure, an over-fed donkey!

. . . .

The picture is still in my mind of that sunny,
undulating April-green field, with its background of trees, with their young spring leaves
twinkling in the sunshine, and the young stal-
lions being led forth in succession, with their
beautiful heads up, stepping so proudly and
delicately, staring at the sleek and elegant
matrons, grazing placidly at the foot of the
slope below them, with their long-legged children tormenting them; and among them the
lovely young mares, soon to make their *début*
on the race-course. What a possession they all
were! No wonder the Tenth Commandment
went to bits!

. . . .

My last act on my last afternoon in Boston

was to pay a visit to Miss Grace Horne's very interesting Picture Galleries, where she was showing an Exhibition of Irish Art (which was not devoid of personal interest for me). It may seem wasteful to have spent the last hour of a very full day in looking at what I had already — to some extent — seen in Ireland. Something of the nature of the Bus-man's holiday, in fact. But it was very agreeable to see Irish pictures assembled and held in honour so far from home. Prophets, not infrequently, are well advised to leave their own country.

.   .   .   .

I have said nothing of the social side of my visit to Boston, because to try and tell of the wonderful time that I enjoyed there appears to me not fitting in a record that I have endeavoured to keep impersonal. To preserve this reticence throughout these memories of our travels has been no easy matter, and there have often been moments when gratitude had to be forcibly gagged! Not even that dinner at the Chilton Club shall be alluded to! I will keep silence, although, as King David said, it is pain and grief to me.

I may at least say that wherever we went, generally, and without distinction of person, our hosts and hostesses made us think of Irish people in their geniality and agreeability, of English people in their consideration and forethought in all things, and of themselves only, in a certain fresh and unconventional outlook on things in general, that has in it the peculiar vitality of a newer world than ours.

CHAPTER XXI

HAD I been transported on the Magic Carpet of the Arabian Nights, or carried blindfold in an aeroplane — (which may Heaven forbid!) — and deposited in the country of the Radnor Hunt Club, and asked to declare where I was, I should unhesitatingly have answered in the English Midlands. Such a bland, rich, comfortable aspect had the scene, and so, equally, did all those warm adjectives befit the houses and 'places,' from Chestnut Hill, and onwards through the country, blossoming in the first fairness of spring.

Broad pasture-fields, rising and falling in pleasant curves, interspersed with tracts of woodland and wooded valleys, and I remember a lovely river, not so wide as to discourage a fox from adventuring it, though swift enough

THE RADNOR HUNT COUNTRY DOES NOT RECALL
WEST CARBERY

perhaps to give pause to his pursuers. As to
the jumps, they seemed, as far as could be seen
from the roads, to be mainly posts and rails;
clean jumping, but to anyone bred to banks
and walls, far from being the most attractive!

At the Radnor Kennels it was cheerful to
find myself again in entire agreement with the
views of the establishment. To my insular
eyes, these hounds, their looks and their manners, would — even as I felt with the Myopia
Pack — be hard to beat in any country, and
their kennels seemed to me to be '*hors concours*,' the last word in that very special branch
of architecture, that is capable, as experience
has shown me, of so many and remarkable
variants — from the organised luxury of a
smart English County pack, such as even the
Radnor hounds might not disdain, to — but
this, I regret to say, was in Ireland — a species
of makeshift den, that apparently served as
general lodging-house and exercise-yard combined. It had in better days been a coach-
house, and from it, that brilliant summer day,
proceeded an odour — (attributable, I was told,
to an unusual diet, consisting mainly of fish,
a fishing village being near) — that I prefer not

to describe, and have in vain struggled to forget.

There may be those so sunken in darkness as, in spite of the preceding mention of the Radnor Kennels, to be unable to open a map of North America and put immediately a finger on that part of the United States at which I had now arrived. For these ignorant ones, therefore, I will say that I was now in the State of Pennsylvania, and the Gospel according to Baily tells us that 'the Radnor Hounds hunt the Delaware and Chester counties.'

Two days earlier I had reluctantly left Boston, sped, even at the austere hour of 8 A.M., by faithful friends (and devotion can go no farther than to 'see-off' a traveller at an hour of which an indignant housemaid has said 'no rale lady'd be out of her bed before eight o'clock in the morning'!). From Boston, I repeat, I pushed on, to pitch my moving tent a day's march farther from home, at Philadelphia, and there I found hospitality as generous and gay as it had been everywhere else, ever since — it seemed so long ago now — we had left the 'Cedric,' and set foot, rather nervously I admit, on American soil.

My first evening in the extremely lively

'Quaker City' not only began with a dinner party, but continued with an entertainment at the fine Opera House, where (among other items) four gentlemen from New York, identical in height, colouring, and costume, strode rapidly on to the stage in single file (so rapidly, indeed, that the silhouette of their evening coat-tails, standing out, in the speed of their advance, straight behind them, has never left me). They then sang part-songs delightfully, ending with a setting for all four voices of 'Old Man River' — then at the peak of popularity — that was entirely enjoyable, and the remembrance of which — like that of the extended coat-tails — is ineffaceable.

Dinner parties had by now become part of my daily routine. From Aiken, to New York, New Haven, Providence, and Boston, it had been Roses, roses, or rather dinner parties, dinner parties, all the way, and I soon found that at Philadelphia the sequence of festivity was not to be broken. And it now occurs to me that if I am to make a protest that has rankled in my bosom from my first American dinner party to my last, I had better do so at once before these records have to cease.

Let me begin by declaring that an especial attraction for me of the American meal, be it lunch or dinner, has been the variety and excellence of its lighter adjuncts of biscuits, toast, brödchen, brioche, — impossible to enumerate them all. Why then, before I have been able to achieve more than a preliminary nibble, have they all been inexorably reft from me? With the retirement of the meat from the scene, a ruthless crumb-brush and tray have ever ravished my most valued crumbs, matters, whether of biscuit, toast, brödchen, or brioche, on which I rely, not so much for actual sustenance, as for moral support in affording occupation during possible pauses in conversation. I have concealed morsels in my lap, (hidden, as it were, my treasure in a napkin) only to forget them, and to be disgraced on leaving the table, by their distribution at my feet.

Diffidently I offer this reproach, and in doing so I am reminded of a tale, (exemplifying a similar, but more serious grievance) that was told to me by 'J. E. P.,' that 'Professor of Embroidery and Collector of Irish Point,' to whom Martin Ross and I dedicated 'The Patrick's Day Hunt.' The story records the moving experiences of a guest, one Mr. Jeremiah Mulrooney, caught up into an unfamiliar sphere, and I think I may venture to summarize it here, since it is not without relevance to the crumpled roseleaf to which I have just alluded, and I have an assurance of its authenticity from the Authority whom I have mentioned.

Not long ago, thus the story begins, Mr. Jeremiah Mulrooney was surveying a farm for me. I came upon him at a moment when a desire for meditation combined with tobacco had temporarily interrupted his labours, and we fell into conversation. I was snipe-shooting, and had some sandwiches in my pocket. I offered him one, and he accepted it. 'Them's nice sangwidges,' he was good enough to observe. 'I'd like a bit o' lunch this way.'

He paused, and ate another of my sandwiches. It appeared to recall to him a past experience.

'Wan time,' he began pensively, 'I was doing a small job o' work for his Lordship, with regard to surveying a share of a bare hill that was occasioning what I might call an acrimonious dispute between a couple of his Lordship's tenants. And it, I may say' — he added — 'without as much on it as'd graze a gandher. Well, it was goin' on for one o'clock when I had me survey completed, and says I to meself, "I'll take me figures up to the Big House before I'll go home."

'What was in it when I gets there but his Lordship and her Ladyship, and they standing on the hall-door steps.

'"Come in, Mr. Mulrooney," says they, friendly and aggreeble, the way I ever knew them. "Come in and have a bit o' lunch," says they, "an' we'll see the map afterwards," says they.

'Well, for all I was in me dishabeel, and dirty old boots on me, I had a scruple to refuse them — (and begor' there wasn't bit nor sup went into me mouth since the dawning o' the day!) — So I thanks them, as in me manners bound, and we went inside to the parlour then and sot down to the table. I seen the big fella of a butler perceiving me boots, and a whipper-snapper of a snap-dragon of a tay-boy that was with him, in red plush breeches and white stockings, was making shnouts at them likewise. But little I regarded them.

'Well, I knew me manners, and I held me tongue, till his Lordship says to me

'"Mr. Mulrooney," says he, "what'll ye ate?"

'"Mate, me lord," says I. (And God knows I was hungry!)

'Well, his Lordship cut off for me then two as nice slices of boiled beef as ever you seen, and a nice little bit o' fat attached, an' he gev it to the whipper-snapper of a snap-dragon of a fella in the plush throwshiers — breeches I should say — an' he puts it down before me.

'I had a nate forkful ready to put in me mouth when her Ladyship addressed a remark to me with regard of pigs.

'Now, swine is a subject I am familiar with, in an' out, from bonnives to bacon, and I puts down me fine forkful, as in me manners bound, to respond to her Ladyship.

'Well, I declare to ye, before you could say Shnipes, the Whipper-snapper of a snap-dragon of a fella in the plush throwshiers — breeches I mane — had the plate whipped away from me!

'I passed no remark. I held me tongue, as in me manners bound, and I was commencing to address a remark to her Ladyship in regard of them fashionable poultry she had that time, when his Lordship sees me idle.

'"Mr. Mulrooney," says he, "you're ateing nothing. What'll ye have?" says he.

'"Well me Lord," says I, "I think I could do no better than have a couple o' slices of that elegant bit o' beef that's before your Lordship," says I.

'With that his Lordship cuts me off two as nice slices as ever you seen, with a nice little bit o' fat attached.

'The owld butler fella puts it down before me, but before I had time to get to come at it, her Ladyship addressed a remark to me in regard of fat cattle.

'Well, out of respects to her Ladyship, and as in me manners bound, I puts down me knife an' me fork before I responds to her. But if I did, by the Gash o' War! if that Whipper-snapper of a snap-dragon of a fella in the plush throwshiers — breeches I should say — hadn't the plate whipped again from me!

'That now was the second time he done it, and says I to meself, "Wait awhile, me lad!" But I held me tongue.

194

'His Lordship then, that hadn't his own dinner hardly begun, and seeing me idle again this way, cuts off another couple of elegant slices for me, with a nice little bit o' fat attached, an' 'twas set down before me.

'Well, listen to me now!' Mr. Mulrooney paused an instant, and fixing me with an infinitely crafty eye, continued his tale with slow emphasis. 'When I reshumed my conversation with her Ladyship in regard of fat stock, I puts down me knife on the table beside me, but I retained me fork in me right-hand, and when the Whipper-snapper of a snap-dragon of a fella in the plush throw — (breeches, I mane, and may the divil sweep them!) — comes around the third time to grab me plate from me, I slews around in me chair, and I says to him, "Your soul to Maurice Kelly!" I says — (for I wouldn't wish to show violence before her Ladyship) — "Move off with yourself!" says I, "ye whipper-snapper of a snap-dragon, before I dam well sink this fork in your dirty fist!" says I.

'Well, with that her Ladyship got very red.'

. . . .

The precaution taken by Mr. Mulrooney

was one on which my mind oft-times dwelt
longingly when the fatal moment of the Brush
and Crumb-tray approached. (And, I may
say, that never did it seem to me a more proper
one than at the admirable luncheon that preceded a visit to the Kennels of the Pickering
Hounds, a specially attractive variety of
crouton having been swept from me in a way
that recalled the epitaph on the infant, dead at
birth.

'Since I was so quickly done for,
I wonder what I was begun for.'

Thus with that delicious biscuit.
But I will leave this painful subject.)

.   .   .   .

The Pickering Kennels are singularly happy
in their position. I should think very few
hounds can have so pleasant a playground, a
big enclosure taken in from a wooded hill, and
Kennels perfectly planned, with such abun-
dant sun and fresh air and space as is not often
bestowed. The Hounds seemed to me the best-
looking of their breed, which is pure American,
that I had seen. They were of the orthodox
three colours, black, white, and tan, with the
long hanging ears (that irresistibly suggest the

portraits of Mrs. Barrett Browning) and beautiful, romantic eyes, and pointed tan toes, that again suggest the poetess, and would look charming in black satin sandals. Again I was struck by their identity of type with our Kerry Beagles, and if I am faithful to the English Foxhound, I can still recognise the beauty of his rivals, and believe in their fitness in the conditions which they are bred to suit.

. . . .

My last memories of Philadelphia are of a whirl of sight-seeing, that ended in a wonderful luncheon with the English Speaking Union, a generous gesture of friendship and hospitality to a wanderer from the other side of the ocean that she will not easily forget.

How I, and my terrible assortment of go-pokes, caught that afternoon train to New York, is a matter known only to that competent Officer of Boy-Scouts, blessedly raised up to my assistance, and to the Benefactress whose motor, panting at the door, awaited the moment when I could tear myself away from my kind hosts, and to yet a third organizer of equally supreme efficiency, who, single-handed, took on the transport of the go-pokes; so that

I reverted with entire contentment to becoming, once more, the effete combination of Baby and Grand Piano.

.   .   .   .

It was typical of the good manners that met us, wherever in the States Fate had led us, that on my arrival in New York, and I stood, in some uncertainty as to the ritual of securing my luggage and a taxi, a gentleman unknown came to my help, volunteering assistance that I most thankfully accepted, and only left me when all difficulties were composed. This was indeed the act of a Good Samaritan, and I should be glad to think that his eye may meet this tribute of grateful remembrance. The date, which was the second of May, is stamped on my memory for more reasons than one, and possibly this may help to recall to his memory his act of charity.

.   .   .   .

The time came, early in May, and came too soon, when 'the painful pleasure of bidding G.B.' had to be finally faced. In order, perhaps, to alleviate it in some degree, (and possibly, also, to reconcile me to turning my back. on New York!) my hostess took me, the night

before I was to start for home, to a play, as
clever as it was horrible, that left me with the
worst impression of New York life that was
possible to receive — '*Street Scene*,' by Elmer
Rice. I can still see the German Communist,
in his shirt-sleeves, haranguing the listless
loafers, still hear the two fateful shots from
the upper story of the shabby tenement house,
and the howling tumult that followed them.
It was all sordid and brutal, terribly well done
— or so it seemed to me, though I suppose
only a City policeman is truly qualified to give
an opinion on the *vraisemblance* of such a
nightmare.

.   .   .   .

But this was not the farewell greeting that
America had for the Irish pilgrim, whose time
of holiday-pilgrimage had come to an end.

> *''Tis hard to part when friends are dear,*
> *Perhaps 'twill cost a sigh, a tear.*
> *Then steal away, give little warning —'*

I wouldn't say that it didn't cost both, nor
that there was not something of a mist before
the eyes that saw the allotted state-room so
filled with letters, books, telegrams, flowers,

and fruit, as almost to leave no space for me and the essential go-pokes!

I had, as the poet enjoins, 'stolen away' and had given 'little warning,' but as the 'Baltic' set her nose for the open sea and Ireland, one good friend, kind representative of the many I was leaving behind me, stood on the shore to wish me Bon Voyage, and to leave me with the happy certainty that the old Irish valediction — 'That your journey may thrive with you!' — which had sped us from our own country, had come true.